ACROSS THE WIDE MISSOURI

The Diary of a Journey from Virginia
To Missouri in 1819 and Back Again in
1822, with a Description of the City of Cincinnati

by

James Brown Campbell

Edited by

Mary Wickizer Burgess

and Michael Burgess

THE BORGO PRESS
An Imprint of Wildside Press

MMVII

STOKVIS STUDIES IN HISTORICAL
CHRONOLOGY AND THOUGHT
ISSN 0270-5338
Number Four

Library of Congress Cataloging-in-Publication Data for the first edition:

Campbell, James Brown, 1798-1852.
    Across the wide Missouri : the diary of a journey from Virginia to Missouri in
1819 and back again in 1822, with a description of the city of Cincinnati / by James
Brown Campbell ; edited by Mary Wickizer Burgess with Michael Burgess.
       p. cm. — (Stokvis studies in historical chronology and thought, ISSN 0270-
5338 ; no. 4)
    Includes index.
    1. United States—Description and travel—1783-1848. 2. Cincinnati (Ohio)—
Description. 3. Campbell, James Brown, 1798-1852. I. Burgess, Mary Wickizer,
1938- . II. Burgess, Michael, 1948- . III. Title. IV. Series: Stokvis studies in historical chronology & thought ; no. 4.
E165.C2 1990   84-268
973.5'4
CIP

SECOND EDITION

Across the Wide Missouri, by James Brown Campbell

CONTENTS

ILLUSTRATIONS

DEDICATION

For "Auntie," with Love

Eugenia Campbell Fidler
(1861-1948)

INTRODUCTION

THE CAMPBELL FAMILY

This account has been transcribed from a typed copy of the original diary of James Brown Campbell, son of Alexander and Margaret Brown Campbell. James Campbell was the oldest of eight brothers who accompanied their parents on a trip from Virginia to Missouri in 1819 and back again in 1822: James Brown, Thomas, John, Samuel Blackbourn, Alexander Hansen, William Mathew, Benjamin Brown, and Edgar. A brief genealogical chart outlining Alexander's family and that of his brother, Samuel Campbell, who is also mentioned in the diary, follows this Introduction.

I have corrected many of the misspelled words, and also some of the punctuation and grammar; but otherwise, and in every way, the diary faithfully reproduces the flavor of the original. Words or phrases added or changed for clarity are indicated by brackets.

Eugenia Campbell Fidler, a granddaughter of Samuel Blackbourn Campbell, had the diary transcribed by her niece, Wilma Evelyn Wickizer (my mother), from an original which had been preserved by Miss Mattie A. Campbell, daughter of Benjamin Brown Campbell. My deepest appreciation and warm affection goes out to these ladies, all now deceased, for their wisdom and foresight. Although I am but a link in the chain, any typographical errors or errors in transcription or interpretation should be laid at my doorstep.

Across the Wide Missouri, by James Brown Campbell

In the summer of 1819, Alexander Campbell and his wife, Margaret Brown, together with their eight sons, servants, and other unspecified traveling companions, departed from their home in what is now Highland County, Virginia, and set forth on a trek into the wilderness of Missouri Territory. It was, perhaps, not such a brave or unusual undertaking as we may now suppose. The Wars of Independence had been concluded, and many veterans and their families had already moved west, seeking land and new opportunities. Alexander and his brother Samuel had moved to Bath County, Virginia a scant twenty years earlier from the Chester County, Pennsylvania/Cecil County, Maryland region, and in 1810, Samuel Campbell (the "Uncle Samuel" mentioned in the diary) moved again with his family to Gallia County, Ohio.

We can only guess at the family's motives, for none are ever mentioned, but certainly the desire for a better future must have entered into Alexander's decision. We are fortunate, at any rate, to have the journal kept by his oldest son, James, to illuminate our surmises.

In 1822, the decision was made to return to Virginia. James himself longed for home and his former companions. He had returned to the family's temporary base camp in Missouri, after a grueling surveying expedition, only to discover his father and brother Thomas had made a sudden, unexplained dash back to Virginia, and that his mother and younger brothers, left alone, were all deathly ill, probably with malaria, dysentery, or the like. He took ill himself, necessitating the only significant break in his journal. When he took up his tale again, the father had returned, and the family was in the midst of preparing for their homeward journey. We never learn why, but can only assume that an inhospitable terrain and an unhealthy climate may have played a major role in the decision. Alexander and his sons never again ventured from the relative seclusion and security of their native Virginia highlands.

It is apparent from the internal evidence of the journal that James Brown Campbell, despite his frontiersman-like prowess, was a sensitive and caring individual, who was rather well-educated for his time. Although his entries seem brief, stilted, and less graceful today than a formal essay would demand, and although there are numerous misspellings and grammatical errors, we must bear in mind that here was a young man barely out of his teens, who, in spite of mind-numbing physical conditions and the backbreaking labor required for his family's survival, managed to write a little bit in his diary each day, and to protect his fragile paper, pen, and ink against a hostile environment. We salute him for his effort to pass on the record of what must have been a fantastic, if at times disillusioning, adventure. His purpose may not have been altruistic; nonetheless, his emotions and observations have here been preserved for posterity.

Across the Wide Missouri, by James Brown Campbell

James had been trained as a surveyor. It is evident from the meticulous records he kept that he was a competent and careful journeyman. His training and natural bent seem also to have resulted in an analytical eye for the details which shine forth from the pages of his journal. He was fascinated with the size, shape, and physical characteristics of things, both the natural and the manmade phenomena he encountered. Streams, bridges, towns, prairies—all are grist for his mill. He tells us, in great detail, the lengths, breadths, and depths of creeks, the weights of objects, the price of merchandise, the numbers of houses, taverns, and churches to be found in each hamlet, the distances between towns, the kinds of trees growing in the forests, and the intensity of rain, lightning, and thunder, during storms. He describes both an eclipse of the moon and of the sun.

It is most unfortunate, however, that he does not extend his attention to detail to the human element. The index to this volume documents the extraordinary number of families and individuals he encountered during his travels. He often fails, though, to include more than a brief mention of the surname. When he attends a wedding at the Bennet[t]'s, for example, he does not mention the given names of the bride and groom, so we have a date, but no participants! When a friend, "Barns," dies, we are not told Barns's first name, although James sits up with him several nights before the end and attends his burial. He does, ironically, give the names of his dog, several horses, and pack animals! The Campbells (of Scotch-Irish Presbyterian background) were a dour lot, and did not, evidently, celebrate birthdays (for such occasions are simply not mentioned), nor do they make much of a to-do over Christmas, although the Fourth of July is duly noted (as are elections, court trials, and races). As might be expected, Sunday preaching and other communal gatherings in neighbors' homes are the most frequent entertainments. He mentions his three next oldest brothers by name half a dozen times, and his parents are mentioned only two or three times, including the occasion of his mother's death, a tragedy so profound, that its account, sandwiched as it is amongst other more prosaic details of the journey home, serves to increase, rather than decrease, its poignancy.

Other anomalies occur. At one point, he is obviously mightily enamored of a Miss Susan Wasson, and spends a great deal of his spare time in her company. The original diary referred to her and his liaisons with her in a crude, easily-deciphered code using numbers in lieu of vowels (which has been eliminated in the interest of clarity). This faintly-disguised attempt to throw potential readers off the track may, perhaps, be attributed to having seven younger brothers residing in a cramped and crowded household. Private property may have been difficult to protect from curious, prying eyes. Later, he seems to have had a fight with one of the Wassons, Susan's brother or father. He leaves on his surveying expedition soon after the quarrel and Susan herself is never mentioned again (although her sister, Nancy, appears to have nursed the family during its illnesses). Did Susan die, or change her mind? Did her father forbid them to meet again? We can only surmise that the love affair soured in some untold way.

We know that Alexander and his sons were slaveholders in Virginia prior to the Civil War. In anticipation of his third marriage, on March 31, 1842, Alexander Campbell deeded three hundred acres of land and eight slaves to his sons, Thomas and Alexander Hanson, retaining the use of them for his lifetime. The slaves are named: "Fanny, called Franky, Adam, Mary, Jesse, Peter, Malinda, Paulina, and an infant at the breast." The following unaccredited account appears in *The Campbell Family History,* compiled in 1973 by Arthur Price Campbell, a descendant of William Mathew Campbell. "Malinda Saunders of Charleston, a servant of Grandfather's and daughter of 'Aunt Frankie,' to whom I wrote says: 'Your Grandpa bought the farm of a man by the name of Pendleton. Mother often spoke of the sad day and how sad it was to start on the road again and leave their Mother behind. They had several horses and cows but one wagon. Mother and the older boys walked and drove the cows; the small children rode in the wagon. I think your Grandpa led the rider-less horse most of the way and I think they kept it until it died of old age. [Your] Grandmother was sick three weeks. *Come Ye That Love the Lord and Let Your Joys Be Known* was the hymn Mother sang by her dying bed. She said she was always a Christian, died happy and she would meet her in heaven.' Aunt Frankie had one child when they went to Missouri, and Adam was born there." It is obvious from the above vignette, that Aunt Frankie was the "black woman" who sang a hymn for Margaret Brown Campbell as she lay dying in Indiana. It is not clear whether any other slaves (other than Aunt Frankie's children) accompanied the family. In any case, the Campbells certainly shared most evenhandedly in the struggle for survival in a hostile landscape. James's younger brothers worked hard, and James, in particular, seems to have taken on a load of responsibility well beyond his tender years. The mention of the rider-less horse adds a further dimension of sadness to an already unhappy tale.

There is another small, inexplicable, yet tantalizing, detail. At various times during the family's return trip, James mentions that curious locals come out to greet them and to "see the elk." The "elk" is never explained. Was it alive? Had they captured and somehow tamed it during their trip? Was it the carcass of a hunting trophy? We can only speculate.

Finally, it is intriguing to note the warm feel of *community* we sense in the diary. Families, friends, and neighbors lived together, worshipped together, and helped each other to plant and harvest crops, raise buildings, cut timber, and to do whatever else was needed in order to survive. It was the accepted practice during one's travels to stop for the night at whatever abode presented itself along the way. Sometimes one paid for a night's lodging and a meal or two, or one didn't, depending, it is supposed, on the need and hospitality of the householder, the solvency of the traveler, and a tacit understanding that if the situation were reversed, one's own home would serve as a temporary refuge for the weary wayfarer. Reliance was placed upon "the kindness of strangers," a reliance which in our own day would be unthinkable, except under the direst of emergencies. In spite of our often-stated notions of a "savage" and violent frontier, it is undeniably clear from James Campbell's diary that settlers on the edge of civilization in his day were very much their "brothers' keepers," and much less prone to wariness and unsociability than the most "civilized" of us can claim to be today.

In conclusion, it is my fervent hope that by recounting James's story, I have also preserved the essence of his spirit and personality. In re-reading this account of the family which anticipated me, I can easily imagine a young man setting out with a mixture of hope and trepidation on an extraordinary adventure of a kind which is denied to most of us today. I am deeply grateful to James Brown Campbell for telling us his tale in a most candid and forthright manner. In publishing this account, to be shared with the descendents of other families who "crossed the wide Missouri," I am attempting, in some small way, to repay our mutual debt to him. We might all take a lesson from his perseverance and steadfastness.

—Mary Wickizer Burgess
Prof. Michael Burgess
San Bernardino, California
13 August 2004

Across the Wide Missouri, by James Brown Campbell

Samuel Blackbourn Campbell
(1804?-1883)

*James Brown Campbell's younger brother, and the second
Great-grandfather of the editor, Mary Wickizer Burgess.*

SAMUEL CAMPBELL
of Gallia County, Ohio

[excerpted from *The Campbell Chronicles*
by Mary Wickizer Burgess]

Samuel Campbell was born circa 1761 in Chester County, Pennsylvania. A pension application states that he was age 16 when he left his father's fields to volunteer for service during the Revolutionary War. He was married on November 9, 1786 in Cecil County, Maryland to Sarah Foster Coulter, widow of Samuel Coulter (born circa 1761; died March 12, 1834). Moved to Bath County, Virginia by February 13, 1798, where he and his brother, Alexander, purchased 130 acres on Back Creek from Daniel and Catharine McGlaughlin for £200; Samuel and Alexander first appear in Bath County personal property tax records on July 28, 1798. Samuel moved with his wife and children to Gallia County, Ohio circa 1810. He died there on March 7, 1841. His family filed suit to partition his estate, providing legal evidence of his surviving offspring. He is buried in the Hulbert Cemetery with his wife and other family members.

The Children of Samuel Campbell:

a. **James**. Born circa 1787 in Maryland. Married Isabella Leech in Pendleton County, Virginia on September 22, 1807. Eventually settled in Tippecanoe County, Indiana where he died, and where many of his descendents lived.
b. **John**. Born circa 1789 in Maryland. Married circa 1810 to Anna ___. Moved prior to his father's death to Adams County, Illinois, where he served as postmaster before his death there leaving descendants.
c. **Margaret**. Born circa 1792 in Maryland. Married May 20, 1813 to John Rees. Lived on the Ohio River opposite Point Pleasant. Died before her father.
d. **Samuel**. Born circa 1794 in Maryland. Married circa 1812 in Virginia to Susan Ross. Married secondly in Gallia County, Ohio on August 24, 1820 to Elenor "Nellie" Waddell. Reverend Samuel died March 20, 1838.

e. **Nancy**. Born circa 1796 in Maryland or Virginia. Married February 13, 1817 to James Graham of Gallia County, Ohio. She died June 16, 1846, aged 49 years.

f. **Elijah F.** Born 1799-1800 in Virginia. Married in Gallia County, Ohio on July 11, 1824 to Nancy Sawyers. Died after 1850.

g. **Elisha**. Born April 5, 1802 in Virginia. Married in Gallia County, Ohio, on July 6, 1826 to Mary "Polly" Waddell. Elisha died April 20, 1845.

ALEXANDER CAMPBELL
of Highland County, Virginia

(excerpted from *The Campbell Chronicles*,
by Mary Wickizer Burgess)

Alexander Campbell was born circa 1767 in Chester County, Pennsylvania; he may have lived for a while in Cecil County, Maryland. Alexander was married on May 20, 1797 in Augusta County, Virginia to Margaret "Peggy" Brown (she was born June 30, 1769, the daughter of Thomas and Elizabeth Crow Brown; she died on June 25, 1822, 12 miles east of Hindustan, Indiana, during the family's return from Missouri). Alexander lived in Bath and then Pendleton County (the part which is now Highland County) until 1819, when he moved with his entire family to what is now Howard County, Missouri. He stayed there 2½ years, then returned to Virginia, settling at the head of Jackson's River. He married secondly, on September 7, 1825, to Mary "Polly" Wandless Moore, widow of Presley Moore (by whom his three youngest children were born); and married thirdly, April 6, 1842, to Rachel Grimes Buzzard (born 1803; daughter of Arthur and Mary Sharp Grimes, and widow of Solomon Buzzard). Alexander died in what is now Highland County, Virginia, about 1845. His will was probated March 17, 1845 (*Pendleton County Will Book 3*, p. 249), and lists his surviving children as heirs.

a. **James Brown.** Born December 1798. Trained as a surveyor, he conducted some of the earliest surveys of the Missouri Territory while his family was living there 1819-1822. He kept a journal of the trip which mentioned many of his friends, acquaintances, and relatives, including his uncle Samuel Campbell's family in Gallia County, Ohio, whom James's family visited during their travels. Listed as a Justice of the Peace for Pendleton County, Virginia in 1831. He married, on June 26, 1845, in Pocahontas County (now West Virginia), to Alcinda C. Lightner, a "noted local beauty" (born circa 1826, daughter of Jacob and Elizabeth Moore Lightner). He appears with her and his half-brother Milton in the 1850 census, listed as a land "speculator." James Brown Campbell died childless in Virginia on October 27, 1852. His will lists his surviving brothers as co-heirs. His widow,

Alcinda, contested the will, forcing a legal response from his next eldest brother, Thomas, resulting in a protracted lawsuit between the Campbell and Lightner heirs extending for years following the deaths of both Alcinda and James.

b. **Thomas**. Born January 21, 1800 in Bath County, Virginia. Married December 4, 1823 to Elizabeth Slaven; married secondly in 1859 to Mary Jane Hamilton Bonner; married thirdly February 9, 1868 to Susan Gum Wade. Thomas died January 24, 1876 in what is now Highland County, Virginia.

c. **John**. Born January 13, 1802 in Bath County, Virginia. Married November 31, 1837 to Sarah "Sally" Johnson. He died in Highland County, Virginia on June 2, 1882.

d. **Infant boy**. Born circa 1803, and died young.

e. **Samuel Blackbourn**. Born circa 1804-5 in Bath County, Virginia. Married June 2, 1828 to Jane Woods; married secondly, on October 25, 1855, to Jane's niece, Isabella Woods. Samuel died November 26, 1883 in his 79th year.

f. **Benjamin Brown**. Born November 18, 1808 in Bath County, Virginia. Married in 1833 to Margaret Slaven (a sister of Elizabeth Slaven, wife of Thomas, above). Married secondly in 1853 to Laura B. Russell. He died March 13, 1884 in Highland County, Virginia.

g. **William Matthew**. Born circa 1811 in Bath County, Virginia. Married on September 21, 1837 to Mary Jane Warwick Mc-Guffin. William died on April 6, 1880 in Highland County.

h. **Alexander Hanson**. Born circa 1816 in Bath County, Virginia. Married on May 16, 1840 to Isabella Spiller Lewis. He died January 30, 1889, aged 72 years, in Highland County.

i. **Edgar**. Born circa 1818 in Bath County, Virginia. Married November 28, 1838 to Susan Herold Boone; married secondly March 30, 1848 to Elizabeth R. Lockridge. He died June 17, 1886 in Highland County, Virginia.

j. **Azariah Perkins**. Born August 3, 1828 in Pendleton County, Virginia. First child of the second marriage. Died of diphtheria on September 17, 1855, aged 27 years, apparently unmarried and childless.

k. **Laura Hamilton**. Born April 18, 1829 in Virginia. Died of diphtheria in October 1847. Mention is made of her unmarked grave in her half-brother James's will.

l. **Milton**. Born September 6, 1831 in Bath County, Virginia. Died in 1861, apparently unmarried and childless.

I.

EIGHTEEN NINETEEN

SEPTEMBER 1819

[At] Laurel Run, east side of Cotton Hill, 6 miles from the falls of Kanawha, September 30, 1819, Thursday evening. It has been my intention to keep a journal ever since I started on this journey but for the want of leisure I have not had an opportunity of commencing it until now.

22nd (Wednesday). We started on Wednesday the 22d of September, our traveling company having come the preceding evening. We were much hurry'd, packing up and arranging our business to leave the country perhaps forever. I sat up the greater part of the night; it set in to rain in the night and continued [the] next morning which made it very disagreeable loading the wagon. There was a crowd of people, almost all our neighbors, there to see us set out, some from one motive, and some from another. After a busy morning preparing, [we] set out about 12 o'clock. It is needless to make any observations on my feelings when I came to leave my native place and taking leave of all my neighbors and acquaintances, no doubt with some of them forever, perhaps with all. In fact I don't know them myself, I had so many different emotions. The day continued rainy and dark, which appeared to give all nature a solemn gloominess much in unison with my [own feelings]. We traveled as far as Charles Hamilton's, 10 miles, and took lodging for the night; part of the family stayed at Squire Hamilton's and overtook us in the morning. Mr. Charles was very kind, and would not charge us a cent.

23rd (Thursday) We delayed starting this morning until we heard from [Mr.] Harold, who sent us word in the night in very pressing terms for us to wait a few days for him and he would go along with us as we had previously agreed on. Mr. Gale went to see him. He returned and brought the news that he could not be ready to go with us. We were then all in a bustle to set off again and got started about 10 o'clock. My reflections today were more gloomy than the day before, having more leisure to consider the journey we were undertaking. Find our load too heavy and the weather like to continue bad. Adam Lightner was good enough to put in one of his horses and help us to the top of the Allegheny mountains where we pitched our tents and camped out for the first night; the weather a little better.

24th (Friday) Got ready and started early this morning in better spirits than since I started. Having gotten another horse of Lightner our load [was] not such hard pulling. Parted with all our neighbors this morning, a great many having stayed with us over night, and got clear of all encumbrances. We have a fair start for the Missouri, a long journey. We drive on 19 miles to Kirkpatrick's on Anthony's Creek and pitch our tents about dark, when in a few minutes it commenced raining very hard, and continued through the night. It ran through our tent and wagons which wet our plunder very much; all who could leave the teams went to the house and barn to lodge.

25th (Saturday) Fed our horses, ate breakfast early and started through the mud; passed over on to the head of Howard's Creek, fell in the state road a few miles beyond the Sulphur Springs situated in Pleasant Valley with a handsome grove of white oaks about the spring and buildings that are erected for the accomodation of visitors to the springs and travelers; the buildings are mostly small, neat, one-storey log houses with two rooms to each, except the dwelling house of Mr. Bowyer who owns the springs together with a large tract of land. I stopped and tasted the water, not so strong a sulphur as I expected nor as other springs that I have seen, it is much the same as the waters of the Augusta Springs in Gennings [Jenning's?] Gap. We went 15 miles and encamped at Joseph Dickson's on Howard's Creek.

26th (Sunday) Started early, went down Howard's Creek some distance, nearly to Greenbrier River which we crossed at a wide ford near 200 feet wide and not more than 18 inches or 2 feet deep; we waited here for one of our horses we had left about a mile back to be shod. Not regarding the Sabbath we drove into Lewisburg and remained a short time there on some business. The road on both sides of Lewisburg is hilly and bad; we came 7 miles out of town and encamped in a hollow between two high hills, somewhat discouraged with the roads. We made 14 miles today.

27th (Monday) Started early in dread of the hills I had to go up this morning; got up very well and proceeded on 17 miles to Alderson's at the forks of the road to Sweet Springs near the foot of Suel [Mountain]. Mr. Alderson has lately come there and has made considerable improvement since he has been there; he is erecting buildings for the purpose of entertainments; he keeps a store there now.

28th (Tuesday) Ascended Suel Mountain, a long steep road, 16 miles to Huggart [Hughart?]. It was some time in the night before we arrived there, when it began to rain and continued through the night.

29th (Wednesday) Still raining this morning; we traveled 4 miles over very rough road to North River, the hills or cliffs are very steep on each side of the river, [and] the road had to be dug 15 or 18 feet in many places to afford a passage for wagons, which is narrow even after digging that depth; the river is rapid and rocky, mostly large round stones, rounded perhaps by frictions in time of high waters. At the ferriage it is 25 and 30 feet deep; the ferry is kept by a Mr. Newman. It was a considerable time before we were all ferry'd over the river, the boat not being large enough to carry more than a wagon and two horses at once; we all crossed however in safety, fed our horses, and took the cliffs on the side of the river which we found worse than [the] side we came down, the road very rocky with short windings; in one of these I overset the wagon which detained us some time. I then left part of my load and went up with the balance to John Vandal's and encamped and packed the rest of my load.

30th (Thursday) This morning I started in good spirits thinking I am over the worst road; we came 3 or 4 miles to a little creek called Wolfpen Creek, which is somewhat of a curiosity on account of its channel. It is a deep ravine in a solid rock near 20 feet deep and almost perpendicular on both sides, it is not over 20 feet across; the road crosses on a wooden bridge, which is built on a crib in the bottom of the creek. There are the remains of a tub mill just below the bridge, built on one of the falls in the rock which affords a good pitch for the water on the wheel. The road from the creek is very steep and rocky for some distance, very difficult for wagons that are coming this way, the rocks some places near two feet high spreading across roads so that horses can't slow up to pull hard. We got up [our] horses with some difficulty and came on to this place (making only 9 miles today), Laurel Creek, where we encamped a few hours before night to dry our baggage and rest our horses before we try Cotton Hill.

OCTOBER 1819

1st   (Friday) Started early this morning over Cotton Hill, the road very bad on both sides; on the west it is dangerous for wagons to come down, the road narrow, sliding and hilly, in many places [so] steep that if a wagon was to overset it [would] go 100 feet one place in particular on the Kanawha in the river cliffs. We make 10 or 11 miles today and encamp on Major Buster's plantation.

2d   (Saturday) Today after a few miles travel we arrive where we have a boat built at Charles Hunter's; some go in the boat, some with the wagons—miles and encamp.

3d   (Sunday) As the river is too low at this place for [the] boat to pass over, we agree to take her empty down as low as the steam mill and there take in our loading; after arriving there we find our boat not to answer a good purpose being too small to take our wagons aboard. We put in our loads however and agree to take the empty wagons by land. Late in the evening we are ready to proceed. We go a few miles with the wagons and encamp. After feeding my horses I start in search of the boat. After going to the river bank I find by enquiring [that] the boat has passed. I then proceeded along down the bank of the river in quest of it; it is a beautiful moonlight night and the prospect along the river delightful, even fanciful, it reminds me of novelistic scenery. I passed a landing for boats at one of the salt works where there was a great many barrels of salt lying on the bank ready to be sent down the river. After walking about 1½ miles I discovered a small fire near the river [and] on coming up to [it], I found [it] to be our company. I stayed some hours with them expecting not to meet them again before we reached Shawnee Town on the Ohio. After making some arrangements I returned to my wagon about 2 o'clock and took a few hours repose by the fire.

4th   (Monday) Started early and drove a few miles to where the road came near the river and waited for the boat to come down.

After it arrived I crossed the river to Charleston, which was nearly opposite to where I had stopped. Charleston is the county seat of Kanawha; it has a good court house and some other scattered buildings. It is situated just above the mouth of Elk River on the bank of the Kanawha. We spent some time here on business and recrossed to the rest of our company. All [are] very much disatisfy'd with the boat. Gale takes a mad caper, resolves to take his load out of the boat and does so, we are compelled to follow his example and leave a fine *bateau* that we had this morning paid $103 for. We then proceeded on to a Mr. Mattick's and encamp, making about 14 miles today.

5th (Tuesday) This morning when I got up I found one of my horses had strayed off. Our company would not wait for us but had gone on and left us. We have hands out in search of our horse and we are waiting his return. He returned about 12 o'clock, we started and went 5 miles to the mouth of [the] Cole and lodged in the house of Mr. Teary.

6th (Wednesday) Started very early this morning, leave the Kanawha River and cross Cole Mountain into Teary's Valley, a good settlement. We proceeded on [to] the Mud River and encamped; made 18 miles today.

7th (Thursday) Continue down Mud River to Guiandott River and encamp at Thomas's after 18 miles today.

8th (Friday) After 1½ miles drive we arrive [at] the mouth of [the] Guiandott. There is a little town of the same name situated on the point between the confluence of the two rivers; its site is pleasant and it appears to be a thriving place. After spending a few hours here we proceed across [the] Guiandott which we forded and along the bank of the Ohio, a very pleasant road and delightful country; cross Twelve Pole River to the mouth of [the] Big Sandy. We had heard before our company was waiting for us, when we arrived they had just left it; they had only gone a short distance to encamp and came back and helped us up the bank of [the] Sandy which is very steep and high; we then encamped altogether ½ mile from the River. Tonight it came on rain and continued till morning; came about 14 miles today.

9th (Saturday) Still raining this morning, very disagreeable. We find the road very bad since we left the Ohio. The present rain makes it much worse for the wagons. I did not drive a short distance before I overset the wagon and had to unload in the rain; very discouraging. We crossed a very bad hill and put up at one Davis's, all wet and cold; only came 4 miles today—almost as disagreeable a day as I [have] ever spent.

10th (Sunday) Started early, the weather cool, cloudy and disagreeable. Crossed some more bad hills [and] encamp at the foot of one very bad one on account of Gale's wagon [which is] likely to break. Came 14 miles today.

11th (Monday) Had [a] hard pulling up the hill this morning, came 13 miles and encamp'd in the woods.

12th (Tuesday) A cool morning. Started early; came 14 miles to Thompson's and encamped.

13th (Wednesday) Left [the] Tyger and crossed over on to the head of [the] Triplet and came down it 10 miles to a Mr. Powers' where we fed; came on 10½ miles further and encamped on the banks of [the] Triplet, well satisfy'd considering we are over the worst road and nearly through the poor settlement of Kentucky.

14th (Thursday) Started early, drove through some good land, beech bottom mostly; some bad mud holes. After about 5 miles travel we arrived at Ilis Mill on [the] Licking River, and crossing it we continued our course nearly west, the road excellent. We cross a dividing ridge on to State Creek and feed; I have to go 1 mile further than the rest to get feed. The road goes up State Creek to the head and then crosses another divide on Flat Creek where we encamp, having come 20 miles.

15th (Friday) We continued across the country, the road hilly. Towards evening we arrive in a beautiful country, the land rich and lying well; we encamp on a hill 2½ miles from Paris [Kentucky], having come 23 miles today and no water near; rain tonight.

16th (Saturday) [A] wet morning, the roads muddy on account of the rain, otherwise good. We drive on to Paris, the county seat of Bourbon. It is situated on a river which has a good toll bridge across it; we forded it however. Paris is a handsome, thriving place, [with] generally good brick buildings. The court house is brick with a tall, elegant steeple which has [a] good appearance as you come towards town. After spending an hour or so here, we continue our course through the rain. It ceased about noon and cleared off in the evening. We encamped in the woods on the banks of [the] Elkhorn, 2 miles from Georgetown. 17 miles today.

17th (Sunday) Drive into Georgetown, the County Seat of Scott, a handsome little town well situated on a hill, not equal though to Paris. In the afternoon we arrive at Frankfort, the seat of government of Kentucky, situated on the banks of the Kentucky River, rather low to be elegant, [with] good buildings and a thriving inland town; we go 4 miles out of town and encamp, having come 23 miles today.

18th (Monday) Today we parted with Bird's family, having come 15 miles and encamped on a little creek, I don't know the name of it. Am writing this by a hot fire and am glad I'm nearly done; got three gallons of cider here for 50 cents. Rain tonight.

19th (Tuesday) Cloudy and cold today; a little rain and looked for snow. We go through Shelbyville, the county seat of Shelby, [which has] a good court house with a tall, elegant, octagonal steeple; the other buildings [are] generally brick and good. 5 miles from here we come to the Bullskin River, which has a long, high, wooden bridge on stone columns across it. We feed here and proceed on to Floyd's Fork and encamp in Jefferson City; 18 miles today. The country we passed through today [is] somewhat rough; good land but hilly, [and] not equal to the lands in Bourbon [county]. The weather cold.

20th (Wednesday) Started this morning after sunrise in fine spirits, the weather pleasant and roads good. In 3 miles we arrive at Middletown, the weather by this time very cold. The road [is] partly paved by a turnpike company who are establishing one from Frankfort to Louisville at an enormous expense, the greater part of which is undertaken at about $25 per rod. We cross Beargrass Creek on an excellent stone bridge with a single span near 20 feet high across the stream. The foundation is a solid limestone rock; there are men at work blowing and breaking the rock to pave the road. Directly after crossing the bridge my team got frightened by the wagon's cloth catching on the limbs of a tree, and in spite of me they ran off with three children in the wagon. They go a considerable distance before we stopped them [when] the off horse fell under the tongue. Two miles further we arrive at Louisville on the banks of the Ohio, which we ferry late in the evening. We encamp on the bank in the suburbs of North Albany, 3 miles from Louisville, a clever little town and the county seat of Floyd on the Indiana.

21st (Thursday) Cold frosty morning, in a few miles we arrive at a high, steep hill called the River Cliffs, crossing which we proceeded through a poor country, thinly settled. [We] go 10 miles to ____ Creek where we feed, after which we proceed 5 miles further and encamp. [We] pass through good land, hilly generally, [with] settlements thin and poor, being newly settled. We pass through Greenville, a little trifling place with a few log houses. I enquired if it was a town and if any person lived in it. It is 13 miles from Albany and has one tavern in it.

22d   (Friday) Started early this morning, the weather cloudy and cold. I have observed this several days—the weather gets considerably colder after sunrise than it is during the night and in the morning before it rises; the wind generally rises as the sun does and continues blowing till it sets. In a few miles we arrive at a considerable prairie with little timber but an undergrowth of oak shrubs. The ground is uneven though not steep, and mostly poor. The wind here [is] extremely cold, [with] nothing to shelter a person from it. We pass several improvements, all new, and arrive at Blue River about 11 o'clock, having come 9 miles. Here we feed and get a bottle of whiskey and 2 lbs. butter (whiskey 25 cents a quart and butter 18-3/4 cents a pound) of one Horner who keeps a little store here. Continue on 14 miles further, the country and settlement nearly the same as what [we] passed in the morning and encamp in the woods having come 24 miles today over a good deal of hilly road. About a mile from Blue River we came to a little town called Fredricksburg containing only a few small log houses. [There were] three taverns in it [but] I did not observe any store at all; it is 12 miles from Greenville and like it, you would not know it was a town without enquiring.

23d   (Saturday) Warm and pleasant this morning after a windy night. [In] 6 miles we arrive at Paoli [Indiana], the county seat of Orange; it has a good stone court house. The other buildings are wood, and there are two taverns in it. We continued on through a hilly country, the road bad, and encamp on a branch in the woods, the water bad. 16 miles today. The water has a bluish cast and stands in puddles in the channel; we are forced to use it for the want of better.

24th (Sunday) The fourth Sabbath since we started, a cold, cloudy, gloomy day, disagreeable traveling. We start early, cross some bad hills, pass a family moving from Tennessee to Missouri. They had the misfortune to lose a horse and are stopped to get another. The country very hilly and roads bad; no water till we get to White County, a town only laid out last summer. It has a tavern and two stores; it is expected it will be the county seat and it is thought by some it will be the seat of government for Indiana. The weather continues gloomy and cold, a little snow, only a few specks however.

25th (Monday) Clear and pleasant. We ford the river this morning; it is 150 yards wide and the deepest place in [the] ford [is] about belly deep to our horses; the bed is a solid rock nearly all the way across, which breaking off abruptly makes a considerable fall in the river, nearly straight across. It is navigable in time of high water above it. There is a keel boat lying just below it now; it is about 40 miles from here to the Ohio River. After crossing one hill immediately after leaving the river, the road is good, the country nearly level; we pass through some very considerable prairies or barrens, having no timber but underbrush. In the evening we come through a very beautiful one. There are several plantations in it and large fields of good corn; it is almost right level and no timber in it at all, not even underbrush; the growth around it is black oak and hickory, [and] the appearance of the soil is near the same as what we passed [through] yesterday. Late in the evening we arrive at Washington, the county seat at present of Daviess, a smart little town [with] 2 taverns and several stores. It appears to be improving smartly. Four miles further we arrive at Little White River and encamp, having come 22 miles today. The bottoms on Little White River are rich and sandy but appear like they mostly overflow. Some considerable improvements.

26th (Tuesday) The weather moderate, the warmest it has been for several days; we drive about a mile along the river and ford it; it is not deep and near as wide as Big White River and like it the bed is solid rock. There is a rapid near the ford and a number of posts in it, I expect for the purpose of taking boats over. The road is narrow and crooked across the bottom and on leaving the bottom there is a short turn in the rock up a little way, where I had some difficulty; had to back the wagon to make the turn. We pass some beautiful prairies like that we passed yesterday, the land rich and level. I observed in one place where there had been some grass mowed, I drove the wagon out of the road to try if the ground was smooth and find it uneven and lumpy, rather [like] tussocks. In the evening we cross a little stream of clear good water, the first running water, except the river, we had seen for some time. It is about 4 or 5 miles from Vincennes; about one mile from Vincennes we come to another little stream called Mill Creek and encamp, having come 15 miles today in Knox County.

27th (Wednesday) The weather continues pleasant. We start early and drive into Vincennes, which is situated in a beautiful and extensive prairie on the east bank of the Wabash. It is a place of considerable trade; it is not compact, [but] is scattered over a considerable space along the bank of the river; it has some good buildings, particularily the Academy which is [a] large and elegant brick building. The steam mill, too, is worthy of notice; there [are] a grist, saw mill and carding machine all worked by the one engine; the grist mill has three sets of burrs; it is owned by a company which purchases all the grain in the neighborhood and sells flour and meal. Flour at present is $3 Cwt. and meal is 3/9 a bushel. After spending a few hours here we ford the river about a mile below town; it is wide and not over belly-deep to our horses, a smooth gravelly bottom and clean water, a beautiful river. We continue down the bank a mile or two, the road narrow and stumpy, the land rich; we then leave the river and go through rich land timbered [with] hickory and black oak; we come to the bank of some river and feed, and shortly after cross [the] Leroy at a saw mill and have a very steep bank to get up out of the river. We then pass through some poor barren lands and in the evening pass through some beautiful prairies and encamp on the edge of one 13 miles from Vincennes, having come 15½ miles today. Have good well water tonight.

28th (Thursday) The weather warm and smoky. We start early; the country nearly all prairie, level and beautiful, many of them on fire. They have a very beautiful appearance, level as far as the eye can reach, with here and there clumps of trees and groves of white oaks. We meet three families this morning moving from the Missouri back to Kentucky. We come 25 miles and encamp on Fox River which is nothing but a nasty pond at this time and is all the water we could get for our horses since morning.

29th (Friday) A little cool and frosty this morning, cloudy and calm. [A] recent fire in the prairie has made it very smoky. We start very early this morning, cross Fox River which has a deep channel and steep banks; the bridge across it not being safe, we ford it and have hard pulling up the bank. A Kentucky team that fell in with us yesterday stalled here and we helped him up. Soon after crossing the river we enter a very extensive prairie, the greatest we have seen yet; it is one continuous plain with scarce a tree to relieve the sight. The day is a little cloudy and very calm and the smoke, settled down very close, obscures the sun. The prospect in this prairie is dreary rather than otherwise. Nothing to be seen but a dusky horizon on every side. After crossing the prairie which is several miles wide, we enter some woodland and shortly after arrive at the Little Wabash which has some good bottom. After leaving it we enter another [yet] more extensive prairie composed of elevated or sloping plains. The first part on this end partly right level. It is 12 miles through it. We come 2 miles through the wood and encamp at Raccoon Creek, which contains no water but puddles, having made 28 miles today.

30th (Saturday) The weather clear and moderate, we start early and in a short distance enter a prairie 4 or 5 miles in extent and nearly right level, and after passing a little skirt of woods we enter another 6 or 7 miles long, and on leaving it we continue some distance in woodland and arrive at Saline River which like most rivers in this state has a deep channel and no water but ponds. There is a man settled here on U.S. land. He says there are three ranges here that have not been sold yet. We feed here, proceed, and soon enter another prairie, which, as usual, has a settler in its edge near the timber who has erected a little horse mill; on leaving it we entered some timbered land, which is rough and the roads bad between the prairies; we cross another prairie and some woodland and enter the Grand Prairie, and 3 miles in it arrive at a little creek which has some timber and encamp, having come 27 miles today; the water [nothing but] puddles.

31st (Sunday) Clear and cool in the morning; start early across the Grand Prairie which is nearly level; the wind blows cold, [and] the road [is] dusty. This prairie reminds me of the account I have read of the deserts of Arabia, being one extended plain and not a stick of timber to be seen; it is a dreary-looking prairie. We cross two drains which have standing water in them. We can, in some places, discover timber at a great distance on both sides of the road which induces one to believe the road goes through it the longest way. It is 23 miles through it the way the road goes. At the west end [it is] a considerable distance from any timber. On a smart eminence there is a well dug and a log hall. For a house there is some kind of a shed for the workmen, made of clapboards and poles; on this hill, at the well (which can be seen at a very great distance on each side from the road), is a handsome site for building but everything is inconvenient. On the west corner of this prairie there are a number of others; on leaving it we proceed some distance through woodland, pass the Shawnee Town fork of the road near the Kaskaskia River where we encamp one or two hours before sundown, having traveled late for several evenings past. The Ocaw or Kaskaskia is a considerable stream, and, I believe, the first running water we have seen since we crossed the Little Wabash. There is a town laid out on its bank opposite to our camp tonight called Carlisle; it is in Washington County. The land was only sold last year and it now contains several tolerable log houses, a tavern and some stores. Came 22 miles today.

NOVEMBER 1819

1st   (Monday) We start at dawn today, the weather cool and pleasant. We ford the Kaskaskia, which is about 15 yards across and little more than knee-deep at this time, yet I am told keelboats have ascended this high. We go through Carlisle which is handsomely situated in the edge of a prairie 6 miles in extent; after crossing [it] we arrive at some woods and cross Stinking Creek on a good wooden bridge. Soon after [we] enter another little prairie which reaches to the woods of Shoal Creek, where there is some good, well-timbered land; we cross it on a good wooden bridge (toll 3/9); the road forks here, one going to St. Louis and the other to Edwardsville; we take the Edwardsville road at the edge of the prairie, which is 6 miles long, passing which we come to Silver Creek and encamp. 26 or 30 miles today. There are little towns laid out in the edge of almost all the prairies. We have passed two or three today I don't know the name of, which have no buildings yet but a few cabins. There is one on the banks of Silver Creek called Augusta, in Madison County. The wind, higher in the afternoon, raises so much dust that together with the smoke, [it] darkens the day; it drives in our faces which makes it very disagreeable. At some times I can't see my horses before me. This appears more like the deserts of Arabia than what we passed yesterday, a dreary disagreeable place indeed. We cast many a wistful eye to see if we could discover the timber along the extremity of the prairie. Very bad stinking odor in Silver Creek; pay 2/3 a dozen for blades tonight. Our company has not got up with us tonight.

2d   (Tuesday) Pleasant weather. We wait some time for our company and are informed by some travelers that the Kentucky team which fell in with us a few days ago ran off and nearly killed Barnes, the driver, and the other wagons [are] now waiting on him; they want us to wait for them. We drive on some distance in woodland then enter a rich prairie several miles in extent; there is a town laid out in the edge of it called Jarvis (I believe). We pass some good lands today and some good settlements; the prairies not so large and more timber. About 12 or 1 o'clock we enter Edwardsville, the county seat of Madison; it is not as good a town as expected. The court house is a small log building. Court [is] in session, [and] I spend some time [there]. The [people here] look generally sickly and very diminutive. We get beef for 6 cents a pound and pay 50 cents for removing a pair of horses. Half a mile from town is Coho Creek where we encamp, the other wagons not having overtaken us yet. 12 miles today.

3d   (Wednesday) I go in search of a horse mill this morning belonging to a Mr. De Lay Plane [Delaplane?]. I follow a small path about ½ mile when I fall into a wagon road at an old water mill and distillery, now dry. I kept along this road ½ mile before I come to any house. Then at a poor cabin I inquire for the mill and by directions I take another blind path which I pursue to a church in the woods which is nearly enclosed by small sheds at about 50 or 60 yards distance. I now began to think I was in Don Quixote's country where I would find nothing but old castles and churches, and after viewing the building, a small frame house with a stove, now occupied as a school house, I set off for my wagon and soon after meet a man. I inquired for the mill and find I am near it, and also that those sheds at the church are for shelters at the camp meetings; it is a Methodist Church and its situation reminded me of the ancient druids. After I got to the mill I could get no meal but got a bag of corn at 50 cents and I then returned to our camp and found the wagon had started, the others having arrived whilst I was gone. I then pass through some hilly land and rough road for a few miles when descending some high bluffs to the American Bottom near a little lake. The road [is] very sandy till near Melton, a little town with several good buildings. The road forks here, one going to Sunbury five miles and the other to Pitcher's Ferry three miles distant. We take the left hand road to Pitcher's Ferry and passing good well-timbered land, we arrive at the Mississippi and pass another little town on its banks containing a few houses, called Alton. We arrive at the ferry about 1 o'clock, the wind too high to cross; we encamp on the bank having come 12 miles today. My team scares and like to run off today again.

4th (Thursday) We begin crossing the river at dawn today and all safely in Missouri in a short time; we continue up the river bottom some distance, the land extremely rich and timber large, being poplar, black walnut, blue ash, hackbury, etc. About 12 o'clock we leave the wood and enter a large prairie, which reaches to St. Charles; we encamp in it two miles short of St. Charles near the house of a Frenchman, having come about 16 miles from accounts but think it much further. The leaves are nearly all off the timber here; a few days since in Illinois they were just beginning to fall in places, later than in Virginia. St. Charles is the seat of justice for St. Charles County, Missouri Territory.

5th (Friday) Weather good. After getting some corn of the Frenchman at 50 cents a bushel, we drive into St. Charles which is situated on the north bank of the Missouri River; it has some good buildings, lately erected, and some of the French buildings yet remaining in it. It has but one street along the river and the bluffs are so close to the river here that there is not room for more. I went down to look at the river for the first time, so long looked for. It is a twisted, dirty looking water, and appears to be unusually low at this time. We spent an hour or so in St. Charles and then proceeded on our journey. The road leaves the river immediatly and enters the high lands or prairies which are hillier and not [as] rich as those in the Illinois. We meet some families moving back today; we are informed of McClintic's death by a man, which is soon after confirmed by three others. It would naturally cause some melancholy sensations to hear of the death of a friend we so soon expected to see after so long an absence, and in a strange country too. We came about 15 miles today and encamp in the woods on the road to the Missouri River, having left the prairie road as we have changed our notion of pushing right to Boone's Licks as was first resolved.

6th (Saturday) The smoke so thick this morning as to darken the day, otherwise clear. We have some difficulty in finding the road; we took a wrong track out [of] the prairie down a steep hill and are obliged to turn back again and then find the road very hilly and bad till we reach the rich bottom. We then continued up it

5 miles to Sumath where [we] arrive about nightfall, having come about 18 miles today.

7th (Sunday) We have not struck our tents today; it being the first since we started; we are holding a council to determine whether we shall winter here or proceed up to Boone's Lick; we have not agreed on any place yet.

8th (Monday) I went a hunting this morning; seen a deer and killed a turkey; the weather is warm and smoky. We have not yet concluded on anything yet. I went to Leonard Harold's today. He lives off the bottom in the uplands.

9th (Tuesday) We concluded this morning to go to Harold's cabins and winter; we start early and drive up there 3½ miles, the road very bad. When we arrive there and see the place, all are dissatisfied and after some parley we turn about and on one of the banks overset the wagon. We go to Leonard Harold's and stay all night having traveled 4 miles.

10th (Wednesday) Warm, cloudy and dark this morning, some rain. We start early in gloomy despondency. Expecting bad weather and dreading the roads, we go down the river to Shoab's and then take up the bluffs and cross over onto Tennsigo Creek, which has good land on it, the bottoms narrow. We pass a Mr. Calliway's [Callaway] and encamp near the head of [the] Tennsigo having come about 14 miles. We meet Armstrong and Kincaid who turn back with us. It rained a little tonight and looks very likely for more.

11th (Thursday) A fine, clear morning. In about 3 miles we reach the state road again, 20 miles from St. Charles. We cross some prairies and rich woodlands and encamp somewhere with 9 wagons, and a cart and carryall. 21 miles on the state road, in all today 24. Very bad water.

12th (Friday) We start at dawn of day, the weather clear and warm. In a few miles we enter a prairie which reaches to the bluffs of Luter [Loutra] Creek, 28 miles from our last encampment. We find deer are plent[iful] in the forests on the edge of the prairie we came through today; we encamp on the banks of [the] Luter. The land here rich and well-timbered; I am told there is a considerable settlement along this creek. The weather cloudy and like for snow, the first winter-like weather for some time.

13th (Saturday) We parley some time this morning considering whether to stop and settle here or not; there are 7 families here from Virginia. We at length start on, all together, the weather cloudy and cold, very like for snow. We soon leave the woodland of Luter and enter a prairie 9 miles in extent and after leaving it we enter timbered land, somewhat rough and hilly but rich and highly susceptible of cultivation, the timber mostly hickory and black oak. There are several families along in the prairie. We encamp on a little creek called the Big R. Arois near the eastern edge of the Grand Prairie and 20 miles from our camp last night at Luter; the weather clear and pleasant, having cleared away about 12 o'clock, warm for the season. I went ahunting this evening; deer are plenty but killed none.

14th (Sunday) Cloudy and cold before noon, looks like for snow; afternoon clear and pleasant, quite warm. We start early and enter the Grand Prairie immediately; it is rolling land and 22 miles through it; at the east edge is a little creek tolerably timbered and then another small prairie two miles in extent. After leaving it the land is well-timbered and rich, [and] lies beautiful nearly to Hingston Creek where we encamp having come 27 miles today. Corn $1 per hundred ears.

15th (Monday) Weather fine; some of our company go on ahead of the wagons to procure a place; the land for some distance from Hingston rough and broken, then rich and well-situated, rolling generally; we cross several creeks today, the names of which I have forgotten. We come 18 miles today and encamp at Mr. Thrall's, where there is a sort of town begun though not laid off. The land here rich and beautiful.

16th (Tuesday) We start early, fine weather, and cross the Moniteau and some other creeks, the land generally good. In about 3 or 4 miles from Franklin, we meet the rest of our company who had gone on to procure a place. They could not get any and were returning without. We cross Sulphur Creek which has high steep banks, hard for a wagon, and continue on to Franklin, Missouri; it was laid out four years ago and now contains a considerable number of small houses and 8 stores, etc; we come two miles out of town and encamp having come 22 miles today.

17th (Wednesday) We drive 6 miles up to Cooper's Fort and encamp, intending to build cabins and rent some land in the prairie. After we are encamped we get dissatisfy'd with the place—

there are two lakes or ponds, one above and one below where we would have to build.

18th (Thursday) I go up to Chariton in search of a cabin; go through the town of Chariton three miles to a Mr. Toolie's where we put up for the night, well-entertained and nothing to pay.

19th (Friday) We start early and go by Ned Morris's. He is a picture of wretchedness; we have some difficulty in finding the way, there are so many paths; after some time we get in the road and reach Cooper's Fort about dark, very tired and have not procured any place.

20th (Saturday) All our company conclude to go up towards Chariton; I am not willing to take the family up there till I know where to go; father goes on ahead of the wagons to look at a little place I had heard of. I start the team and drive as far as Becknel's Salt Works and encamp waiting my father's return. The weather today is dark and gloomy, very like for snow, which would make us more wretched in our unsheltered condition; a pensive melancholy darkens every countenance; about dusk father returned with the news that he had got the promise of a cabin and small improvement, the cabin very small, yet the prospect of a home, though a temporary one, seems to revive us and we look forward with delight to the end of our wanderings.

21st (Sunday) Another Sabbath smiles upon us, the weather having cleared off; we start to our expected home, reach it in the evening. We find the cabin as small as we expected, only 12 feet square; a miserable hut, yet any shelter like a home after so much wandering about is agreeable and we enter it with pleasure; a pleasure however of a very short duration, for not having made any bargain with Mr. Andrews, the man who has possession of our place, he came down about dark and told us he had promised to let another man have it, provided he could not suit himself better against Thursday next; and he would not agree that we should have it till he knew. We could not prevail on him to rent it to us, yet he wished us to wait till [he could] see whether the other man would take it or not. Andrews is late from North Carolina and I think he is one of the monsters of creation.

22d (Monday) The weather is fine, but we are all here in a wretched situation; we don't know what to do; the season has long since arrived that we may expect winter; we have no place or kind of a shelter provided nor have we any prospect of getting any; some of the children are sick; our reserves are wasting fast; we are entirely amongst strangers and from the little acquaintance we have with them can not have any high opinion of them. It is the most wretched, inactive state we have yet experienced. Mr. Andrews has been to see us again this morning; it was dark when he was here last night and I had not a view of him; he is a little onery-looking man and too insignificant to be a monster as I said yesterday, yet I believe he is a sordid little wretch and a man without a heart; he has sort of given us grant of the place which is a little comfort. I have never thought seriously of home till now, and when I contrast our once-happy with our now-miserable condition, it awakes the most painful emotions. Nothing is so mortifying as being dependent on a wretch, and to solicit for this miserable hound. I read the poem on hope with some degree of satisfaction:

Hope unyielding to despair
Springs forever fresh and fair.

etc. It seems to suit our situation. Whilst walking over the place and ruminating on the past in a kind of melancholy, I chanced to find a small piece of snake root which accidentally remained in my waistcoat pocket and on such trifling things depends man's happiness; that this had a wonderful effect on my mind when I consider where I got it, who I got it of, and the happy situation I was then in a thousand miles from here; it awakes the keenest sensations I have ever yet experienced, reflecting too that they are fled forever makes them more so. Andrews has been down to see us tonight and [agrees to] rent us this improvement. He asks an enormous price for it; he sees our necessity and takes advantage of it, which makes my conjecture true, that he is a man without a heart. We are obliged partly to agree to his terms.

23d (Tuesday) I go to help Andrews today, who is about building a distillery.

24th (Wednesday) We begin to cut logs to build a cabin; find some already cut, haul a few together.

25th (Thursday) I went out ahunting this morning and killed a fawn, the first game I have killed since we stopped; it happened seasonably too, for we are out of meat. It began to rain early in the morning and continued through the day, cold and disagreeable. We can't work at our cabin; are obliged to keep our horses tied up in the rain; at night we venture to turn them loose in the field after hobbling the most of them.

26th (Friday) Cold, cloudy and disagreeable, a little rain in the morning, as gloomy a day as the latter end of November can produce, which adds to the gloom of our situation. We work a little at our cabin. I went ahunting again today and killed a fine fat doe, another seasonable supply.

27th (Saturday) Clear and very cold this morning; we continue doing a little at our cabin. I went this morning to bring in my deer and not getting there before night, I was unable to find it, and had a disagreeable time in the brush, very cold.

28th (Sunday) A clear fine day, another smiling Sabbath. Father and brother Thomas went to Chariton to preaching; they say there was a good sermon delivered to a numerous and respectable congregation. I spent the greater part of this day in writing a letter to Jacob Harding.

DECEMBER 1819

1st (Wednesday) Winter has ushered in pleasantly, the weather very warm for this season of the year; I have heard it said the three first days of December govern the winter and if so it will be a warm one. We are still working at our cabin.

5th (Sunday) The weather warm, it has been warm all last week; today cloudy and much thunder. We forbode approaching winter in the evening and at night a considerable rain. We have been working all week at our cabin.

6th (Monday) Partly clear and not very cold, a little uncommon for it to clear off warm this time of the year.

10th (Friday) Cloudy with a little rain. We completed our cabin today with a mud back wall. I went to one Cruze's to sell him a horse.

14th (Tuesday) Clear and not very cold. I start to Franklin to go out to the Buffalo Lick on the Bon Femme, a handsome country there, the land rich and well-situated. I put up at Richmond, a little town laid [out] this last summer and has but one house in it yet.

15th (Wednesday) Clear and cold, winter-like weather. I proceed on to Franklin, taking [in] Toolie's [on] the route. I put up at Prichard's Inn, entertainment not very good and if I may judge of Franklin from what I see here, it is a very dissipated place much given to gambling.

16th (Thursday) I await this morning for races to commence in expectation of seeing Cunningham at them; he did not come and [I] came up to Cooper's Fort, and from thence home a little after dark.

17th (Friday) I went to Jackson's to enjoy corn.

18th (Saturday) It began to snow before daylight and continued through the day, without intermission, to snow very fast. It has fallen to the depth of near a foot.

19th (Sunday) Cloudy and cold, the snow hangs on the trees; it appears like the winter has set in, in earnest. I went to preaching today, the first I [had] been at since I left Virginia. The congregation was small, I suppose on account of the coldness of the weather. An old grey-headed man preached who is not very well-qualify'd for the task.

20th (Monday) Went to [the] mill to grind, but it being too thronged we came back without; in the evening I went out to hunt and was so unlucky as to mistake my dog for a deer, and leveling my rifle with too fatal a certainty, I gave him a mortal wound. The poor fellow cry'd out most piteously and ran off a few paces and soon died, [having] been [hit] near the heart. This grieved me more, perhaps, than a more serious misfortune would have done; he was a faithful and good animal, and follow'd us from Virginia, near 1000 miles, to die by the hand of his master.

21st (Tuesday) Quite warm today, the snow has nearly half thaw'd away. I went out ahunting again this morning but killed nothing. I could not resist a desire to go and see my poor dog Teague, having left him yesterday before he died, as I could not bear to stay with him, and yet cherishing the hope (tho' vain) that the wound was not mortal; on coming to the place I found [him] stretched in the snow, dead and part of his entrails pressed out at the wound, a melancholy sight to me. I laid him by the side of a log in the snow as the last mournful tribute to a faithful friend and left him forever.

22d (Wednesday) Cold, a little snow and rain.

23d (Thursday) Extremely cold, cloudy, etc.

24th (Friday) Continues cold and dull.

25th (Saturday) Clear and moderate today. A pleasant Christmas. I went to Jackson's today, [and] at night to a ball at Andrews'.

26th (Sunday) Pleasant; I went to Chariton to preaching today.

27th (Monday) Moderate.

28th (Tuesday) Extremely cold; I go to Craig's Salt Works, [but] get no salt.

29th (Wednesday) Cold morning, evening moderate and cloudy.

30th and 31st (Thursday and Friday) Excessive cold.

II.

EIGHTEEN TWENTY

JANUARY 1820

1st (Saturday) A little moderated since yesterday. I go to Mr. Yates' for a hog.

4th (Tuesday) I start to Mr. Toolie's.

5th (Wednesday) Went to Franklin, clear and very cold. At night I stayed at a Mr. McKenny's, near the salt works.

6th (Thursday) Got 60 lbs. salt and returned. The weather moderate; at night I go to Mr. Andrew's and stay all night.

7th (Friday) Went ahunting, killed nothing; the weather warm and thawing.

8th (Saturday) Continues warm; went to Mr. J. Jackson's and got 12 bushels corn.

9th (Sunday) Snows all day, very fast.

10th (Monday) Cold and a little snow.

11th (Tuesday) Excessive cold; go to mill today and grind six bushels, nearly freeze too.

12th (Wednesday) Continues cold.

13th (Thursday) Clear and moderate. Buy Turner's hogs today, for $2 a head, 28 head.

14th (Friday) Stormy and snow.

15th (Saturday) Continuous snowing.

16th (Sunday) Snows very fast today.

17th (Monday) Continues to snow a little, cold.

18th and 19th (Tuesday and Wednesday) Cold and dull, some snow.

20th and 21st (Thursday and Friday) Continues much the same.

22d (Saturday) Clear and cold.

23d (Sunday) Clear, cold and frosty air.

24th, 25th and 26th (Monday, Tuesday and Wednesday) A little more moderate.

27th (Thursday) Cloudy and cold, a little snow in the evening. Go to Craig's today and from thence...

28th (Friday) to Franklin and at night to a Mr. Jourden's [Jorden's]. Snow about 2 or 3 inches deep tonight on the old snow.

29th (Saturday) Go through the hills to Cooper's Fort; partly cloudy and dull, thence to a McCafferty to [the] ferry, and to a Mr. Richie's and lodge there for [the] night.

30th (Sunday) Clear and very cold. Try for a school; too late to come home, [so] I return [to] Mr. Richie's.

31st (Monday) Clear and cold. I go up through Richland bottom to the head and lodge at a Mr. Ligget's on the bank of the Missouri.

FEBRUARY 1820

1st (Tuesday) Excessive cold morning, a smart wind. I cross the Hurricane [Creek going] home and feel its effects. Moderate in the P. M.

2d (Wednesday) Continues moderate.

3d (Thursday) [The same...]

4th (Friday) Quite moderate, thawed today.

5th (Saturday) Continues warm, snow thaws fast. I go to take a bee tree, very sloppy walking.

6th (Sunday) Gloomy and cloudy, not very cold.

12th (Saturday) The weather has continued warm and thawing; I go to G. Jacksons', Esq. to a trial between Andrews and E. Waldon, which is decided, contrary to my expectation, in favor of Waldon (the defendant).

13th (Sunday) Weather much the same. Kincaid, Mann, and J. Armstrong come here this evening and stay till morning, which affords a kind of melancholy pleasure, to meet with random acquaintances. Kincaid is on his way moving down to Beth.

14th (Monday) Dark and gloomy, rendered more so by them leaving us. At night go to a Valentine drawing.

15th (Tuesday) Go to Franklin to the race of the two Whips; [the] young Whip wins.

16th (Wednesday) Return home by way of Richmond in company with Birch and Pallet. John Gall stays with us tonight. Walked about midnight by Frank Sendang's; out. Windy and freezing tonight.

17th (Thursday) Clear and pleasant. (Melancholy.)

19th (Saturday) High wind, otherwise clear and pleasant. I went this morning to survey a piece of ground for John Waldon and received for it $1.12½, being the first I have received since I have been in the territory. A sum so small, and in itself insignificant, reminds me of Dr. Franklin's observations on receiving his first wages when he set up his trade in Philadelphia.

20th (Sunday) Went to Mr. Morris to preaching, a considerable con-gregation. Mr. Rogers, an Englishman, preached.

21st (Monday) Windy and clear; (a slight cold).

26th (Saturday) Cool and windy. It has continued quite moderate since the 4th or 5th inst. I go to a log-rolling at R. Wasson's, [and] a ball in the evening [with] pleasant company.

27th (Sunday) Clear and pleasant. I go to Hurricane Creek and call at Wasson's.

28th (Monday) Very warm; haul a load of corn from J. Jackson's, 22 bushels.

29th (Tuesday) Very warm for this season; as the first day of this month was excessive cold, so the last is as much on the opposite extreme, very warm.

MARCH 1820

1st (Wednesday) Clear and warm, windy as generally has been the case since the breaking up of the hard weather.

2d (Thursday) Cool; finish my plough[ing] after a week's work.

3d (Friday) Disagreeably cool without my flannel, clear and windy.

5th (Sunday) Cool; went to preaching to George Wilson's and in the evening to Mr. Wasson's and from thence to Elisha Witt's and stay there all night.

6th (Monday) Start home early in company with _____ very cold today.

7th (Tuesday) Went to Brawley's Mill and grind 8½ bushel corn. Cold.

9th (Thursday) Still continues cold; went to look at J. Martin's place.

10th (Friday) Work on the roads, cold.

11th (Saturday) Snowing very fast and cold.

12th (Sunday) Snow several inches deep; we track up some stray hogs in it.

13th (Monday) Continues cool, some snow on the ground, and yet I go to Franklin the fifth time and to the first Court; lodge at Menis' tavern; good entertainment. Some rain at night, snowed.

14th (Tuesday) Cool morning and then pleasant. I attend court, [a] large collection of people there; meet with W. Mann in town, and come home in company with him by Mr. Fall's where we stay all night.

15th (Wednesday) Return home; find a bee tree on the road. Warm, etc.

16th (Thursday) Go take my bee tree and look at some land. I find another bee tree.

17th (Friday) Go take [the bee tree]; father goes to look at the land. Warm.

18th (Saturday) Warm and windy.

19th (Sunday) Go [to] Mr. Morris's to preaching, large congregation. Whilst looking over them with indifference as I thought, my eyes were invaribly drawn to a particular place, and there they would encounter those of _____. Pleasant day. Return home early, somewhat moody; at night go alone with Pallet, Jones, and Crews [Cruse?] to Sugar Camp, [but] not much pleasure.

20th (Monday) Cool but pleasant; go to Sanford's to see if Gall had passed [through]; shortly after I return home, Gall and Armstrong arrive on their way, moving. Seeing them revives those remembrances of former times, which create a kind of mingled emotion of pleasure and pain; the latter appears most to predominate.

21st (Tuesday) Go to Perry's to make rails.

22d (Wednesday) Begin to make rails and split 300 today, me and [brother] Thomas.

23d (Thursday) Go to help Wassons roll logs.

24th (Friday) Return to Perry's early and finish making rails today (712 rails).

25th (Saturday) It began to rain last night and continues raining today. Suppose this to be the equinoxial storm; it has rained very steady all day with very little intermission.

26th (Sunday) It has continued to rain all last night; this morning, a while before day, the wind blew extremely hard and dashed the rain against the roof of the house with great force and noise. A wonderful storm of wind and rain. This morning it is dark and gloomy, no rain yet, but it has the appearance of not being over, somewhat cool. It has continued raining today at times, some hard showers.

27th (Monday) Clear and pleasant, a beautiful spring morning. I go to Findley's to look at a milch cow; don't see her and go from thence to Hammond Morris's and engage to work ½ month for him.

28th (Tuesday) Me and [brother] Thomas go to work for Morris.

29th (Wednesday) I returned home yesterday evening from Morris's, and today haul a load of corn from J. Jackson's, 16 bushels. Quite cool today. At night I start back to Morris's and go as far as Wasson's, and have the pleasure of Miss Susan's company, late.

30th (Thursday) Start at dawn of day to Morris's; very cold this morning. Finish his clearing today.

31st (Friday) Cloudy and warm; continue to work for Morris, making rails. P. M. clear and sultry. Return home late.

APRIL 1820

1st (Saturday) Cold morning. Have to attend muster, grows colder, some snow and very cold in the afternoon; a great change since yesterday. This is the first muster I have been at in the Territory. The appearance of [the] officers and company [is] not calculated to inspire very high ideas of respect and esteem. [The] officers [are] very meanly-dressed and display no abilities.

2d (Sunday) Clear and cool. Easter Day. Pay Miss Susan a visit and return home before night.

3d (Monday) Start to Morris's early, cool morning.

4th (Tuesday) Still cool, frosty night.

5th (Wednesday) Continue to work for Morris, clearing ground today. Finish working for him and receive $10 for 13 days work. Return home by Findley's, warm, etc.

6th   (Thursday) Cool morning; start to Wilhite's or Crigler's to make rails. A shower of rain this evening, [and] we get all wet.

7th and 8th (Friday and Saturday) Finish making rails for Crigler; have made a thousand since dinner Thursday (me and [brothers] Thomas and John).

9th   (Sunday) Start home after breakfast; come by Andrew's Distillery and meet a number of women going, and Miss Susan among them. I go to Andrew's tonight and have the pleasure of Nancy's company.

10th (Monday) Return home early; [a] pleasant morning, a little cool and windy, as is generally the case. We go to R. Wasson's and rent 5¼ acres of ground option at 2½ barrels per acre. After returning home, we find Miss Susan and her sister, who remain nearly all day and I then accompany them home.

11th (Tuesday) Help John Waldon roll logs, return home late in evening.

12th (Wednesday) Roll our own logs and make a pair of moccasins.

13th (Thursday) Sow flaxseed today, [and] help Andrews roll in the evening.

14th (Friday) Rainy morning, after which it is dry till night; we go to mill and grind 4½ bushels [of] corn.

15th (Saturday) It rained very hard nearly all last night and there was much hard thunder; it has continued raining very fast in the morning and all day with short intermissions. All the branches are much swollen.

16th (Sunday) Warm; attend preaching at Thomas Morris'. Two sermons delivered by two strange preachers and an exhortation by Mr. Thorpe.

17th (Monday) Go to make rails for Mr. Ford.

19th and 20th (Wednesday and Thursday) Showery and very disagreeable.

21st (Friday) Clear and pleasant. Vegetation has made great progress during the present week, trees putting forth leaves and the ground quite green, plenty of grass in the woods now for stock. Return home this morning from Ford's and have been reading *The Vicar of Wakefield*, a new thing to me. I have been pleased with all the works of Goldsmith that I [have] seen; I find this not less interesting than his other works; it has more good sentiment than is generally found in such works and has much of [the] ways of the world in it—since writing the above I have perused it satisfactorily. I find many of the scenes rather unnatural not so much for being overdrawn as [for] coming up to nature. Still it abounds with philosophical observation and has something of the world in it.

22d (Saturday) Clear and warm; plant sweet potatoes today.

23d (Sunday) Clear and warm after a shower last night. Mr. Burch [Birch?] visits us today; I walk home with him and return late in the evening. Very warm.

24th (Monday) Clear and pleasantly cool; begin to mark out for corn.

25th (Tuesday) Stopped by a shower of rain, out all evening.

26th (Wednesday) Clear and warm. Begin to plant this evening.

27th (Thursday) Plant field about the house in corn today. See Miss Susan here.

28th (Friday) Mark out ground at Wasson's.

29th (Saturday) Plant here. Samuel [brother] sick.

30th (Sunday) A fine day. Take a walk to Kinsey's and Morris's and to _____.

MAY 1820

1st (Monday) Go to Chariton to the election of conventioners.

2d (Tuesday) Haul 20 bushels of corn from Paddy Woods', return at night.

3d (Wednesday) Go to Franklin; a great many people [are] there [for] the last day of the election. I go home with the Reverend Mr. Thorpe [to] Cooper's Bottom, 8 miles from Franklin.

4th (Thursday) Return to Franklin again and then home with Williams and Wasson & _____.

5th (Friday) Work for Perry.

6th (Saturday) Finish planting corn.

7th (Sunday) Cool and cloudy after a thunderstorm and rain last night.

8th (Monday) Help Perry peel bark.

9th (Tuesday) Go to mill, [but] can't grind. Begin Perry's plow[ing].

10th (Wednesday) Go to mill and grind; horses run off.

14th (Sunday) Start to Cedar Creek, cross the Bon Femme, Salt Creek, [and the] Moniteau, etc. Stay all night at one Wilhite's 4 miles from Thrawl's.

15th (Monday) After breakfast, proceed on to Thrawl's. [I] inquire the way there, then proceed through some very rough poor land, cross the Persia by Caves', fall into the new cut road near Smithton. Put up at Harris's on said road; he is from Madison in Kentucky and is acquainted with [my] uncle, John Brown. He informs me [Brown] is coming to this country. *[Editor's note: John Brown, Margaret Brown Campbell's brother,* **did** *leave Madison County, Kentucky, but died before reaching his destination.]*

16th (Tuesday) Wait for breakfast (not having supped), pay my bill, 75 cents, and proceed cross the lower end of the 2 mile prairie; it looks handsome this time of year, being covered with a verdant rug of green interspersed with different colored flowers. The day was cloudy, which gave it rather a gloomy appearance; it is about 4 miles across the prairie at this place. Soon after our leaving it, it began to rain which continued till [we] crossed [the] Cedar and reached Henderson's where I put up. In the evening it moderated and I go to one Holt; I take a wrong path on returning and am bothered till [I] give [the horse] the rein and [he] brings me straight to Henderson's.

17th (Wednesday) The rain pours down in torrents this morning and did nearly all last night. I cannot stir out but am confined to the house, and am writing this to amuse me, as there [are] no books, and only the company of young ladies to beguile the tedious hours, which, not being very interesting, I find [time] hangs heavy. It continues to rain until night, such a day's rain I think I [have] never seen before.

18th (Thursday) A dull wet morning; I go to Holt's and with him to the lick as [it] has cleared off and then to the Round Prairie through some hard lands. Survey some for Holt.

19th (Friday) Finish his surveying and go with him to Cliffton's, who lives in a little bottom on a branch of [the] Cedar, [and] whose hills [have a] striking resemblance to Back Creek [Virginia]. I then go to [the] mill, cross [the] Cedar and go to Jacob Zumatt's; stay there all night; expect to survey some for him.

20th (Saturday) I am disappointed about surveying; he goes to a raising. He directs me where I may ford [the] Cedar; on attempting it I find it too deep and [am] obliged to swim my horse over; have some difficulty in getting up the bank. I got all wet and am now drying myself. [At] 10 o'clock, [I] proceed on down through the bottom towards the village of Cote Sans Dessein. Stop at General Ramsay's and feed (6 miles from [the] village and the last house but one in the bottom); above it I see two keel-boats pass up the river while here, which acclaims [provides] me with a [front-view] seat on the river. I cross the Revaws, which is deep, and proceed on to the village which is composed of a few French huts scattered along the margin of the river, about ½ mile below the hill, which [gives it] its name. The hill [is] somewhat of a curiosity; it is 1½ miles long. On one side the base is washed the whole length by the river, [and] at the lower end it rises gradually for about 60 or 70 yards, then continues nearly level along the top to near the other end, where the descent is a little more abrupt but not steep; it is composed principally of hard flinty rock and clay, unlike the plain around it. The breadth of the base doesn't appear to be more than 40 yards at any place and maintains nearly the same breadth the whole length. It is entirely covered with timber and is unconnected with any other high ground. The bottom is wide and high, meets the hill and river and falls off towards the bluffs and is low and wet; where the village stands is a handsome site for a town, the river running nearly above and below for a considerable distance. I put up at Dunica's; John Dunica is an intelligent young man and gave me much information.

21st (Sunday) Like for rain. I start for Henderson's, turn off to Prince's, then to the Round Prairie and am lost nearly all day; reach Henderson's in the evening, much fatigued.

22d (Monday) Go to look at some lands with Mr. Henderson, to Murray's and Hall's; in the evening run a line for Henderson.

23d (Tuesday) Go to J. Zumatt's to survey for him as I had previously agreed; he has started to St. Louis. I am again disappointed, my hopes of making a trifle blown up to the moon; I am much vexed. I can't help secretly cursing him for disappointing [me]; I can't help myself however. Start to Captain Ramsay's, part of the way through the somewhat melancholy woods. I suppose I am now near Ramsay's; I can hear the cocks crowing; I proceed and soon reach Ramsay's, [but] he is not at home. I [then] inquire the way to Nashville, [and] go as far as John Wood's. He has some surveying to do, but will employ me with W. Ramsay; will I go there? [Ramsay] doesn't wish his run at that time but sends me back to his father's, the Captain, who, he assures me, will have *his* run. I go there and stay all night, [but] he has nothing for me to do. I start after breakfast, [and] go [back] to Woods', who, finding I had not surveyed for Ramsay, would not have his done, distrusting, I suppose, my abilities, or thinking it not legal without [a] county surveyor. Some men have the knack of turning the ignorance of people to their own advantage. But I find it has generally been a disadvantage to me; damn his ignorance—nothing but disappointment! I proceed on to Nashville, feed at Walker's, cross the little Bon Femme, go to Cunningham's, then to Titer's and put up for the night.

24th (Wednesday) Rain last night, cold and gloomy morning. I lie late [and] don't start till after breakfast but don't eat any. I then go up by a horse mill to cross the Persia, fall in company with a McCreary, pass Lientz's and Thrawl's, then go to Wilhite's and eat my dinner with a good appetite having [eaten] no breakfast. Nothing to do here, disappointment has grown familiar. I wander across the country till night and fall in at a Captain Owens, fare good, nothing to pay. Owens is one of those good kind of men so rarely to be found.

25th (Thursday) Go to Burckhartte's lick, thence to Richmond and home; tired riding as I now am of writing this.

26th (Friday) Clear and cool.

28th (Sunday) Some rain. I went _____ etc.

JUNE 1820

3d (Saturday) Nothing particular has occurred since my last entry; my time has been generally spent in doing little or nothing, disagreeable lassitude. This morning I started to Bluffton in company with brother Thomas and W. Andrews. The weather is fine. We cross the Chariton about 8 o'clock which presents another appearance now than when I last seen it; it was then not more than a few yards across being very low; it is now about 150 yards at the ferry just below the fork; the Missouri is high at this time and backs the water of Chariton for some miles which causes its formidable appearance. We proceed through the bottom between the Missouri and [the] Chariton for 7 or 8 miles; there is no settlement, then there are some large improvements to the edge of the prairie about 4 or 5 miles further which reaches in to the Military bounty lands. Some good lands near the edge of the prairie. From thence there is no timber except a skirt along the river for about 4 miles to a little creek called Parmers Branch, along which there is a grove of timber to its source in bluffs not more than a mile off. On crossing this branch we again enter the prairie which is level and rich (being the river bottom) and appears to be well-calculated for cultivation. There is a skirt of timber all along the river on the left and on the right we discover the bluffs rising above the plain, and covered with timber which has a very striking and beautiful appearance. They present to the view many handsome sites for building and look as if nature formed [it] expressly for that purpose, with the rich, open plain in front stretching, far and wide, and bordering on the river. It requires but little aid of the fancy to convert every one of those [sites] into a gentleman's seat, with groves, orchards, meadows, etc. This prairie reaches to [the] Grande River with very [little] difference in its appearance. [The] Grande River is 25 miles from [the] Chariton; it is somewhat larger and, like it, is much raised at present with backwater; the ferry is near the mouth. On the west side of the river there are a few miles of timber and it is about 12 miles further to the Waquenda [Wah Ken Dah] Creek; here we encamp for the night. The Waquenda is a small creek, but like the other waters, empties into the Missouri, much backed up now. We [go] 9 miles up it before we can cross without swimming, which is proof that the country is extremely level, and should, [I] think, [be] rather unhealthy where there is so much backwater. There is but a narrow skirt of timber along this [stretch], [with] hills and broken land on your right; on your left [lies] an extensive level prairie. There are several families settled along in the timber who mostly cultivate land in the prairie.

4th (Sunday) We start early, cross [the] Waquenda, and are immediately in the big prairie, which, like the other, is in the river bottom and is very level. About 2 or 3 miles from the Waquenda there is a handsome grove of large black walnut timber, in near a circular form, of about a mile in diameter. Soon, after passing this, you discover, at a great distance, a little clump of trees, the top of which are just visible above the horizon which appears in your sight by slow degrees; this is called the Round Grove, and is about the size of the former [prairie], and about 15 miles from it; [it] is a sort of beacon (as well as [a] meeting place) for travelers, as there is no other timber discernable in that direction till you travel many miles from this grove. It is about 8 or 10 miles to the timber on Crooked River. It is about 30 miles through this prairie, with scarce a single break in the whole; on the left there is timber all along the river (which is called the Sugartree Bottom). On Crooked River there is some good bottom, well-timbered; we ferry'd the river and then went through a small prairie to the river, to one Turner's, and stay all night.

5th (Monday) Go to Bluffton sales. On leaving Turner's this morning we continue through [the] bottom which is good soil and better-timbered (with large oaks) than the Missouri bottoms generally are. Coming to a branch not more than 10 or 12 yards across, we find it too deep to ford and swim our horses over it. When the river is low, I am told, there is scarce any water in it and [it] is raised now altogether by backwater, a [further] proof of the levelness of the country. We reach Bluffton about 10 o'clock; it is named from its situation, the bluffs putting in close to the river. It is a good site for a town, a considerable elevation which commands a handsome view on the river; it is in an angle of the river, bearing south. The only landing is rather below the town. [At] 12 o'clock [they] commenced selling lots which I think sell high for a new place with not a house finished in it yet; about $80 and $90 average. Rain this evening. Having hampered our horses and turned them out, they break their hobbles and we have to hunt them in the rain; very disagreeable. We find them near one Wells', about two miles from Bluffton; we hobble them and again turn them loose, and stay at Wells'. Rains very hard.

6th (Tuesday) Some rain this morning. Hunt our horses till near 12 o'clock, then start up to Fishing River. We come into the Missouri bottom which is wet and muddy, owing partly to the late rains; in a few miles the road comes near the bluff and the land is high and dry, which is rather singular for the Missouri bottom to be high next [to] the bluffs; the soil [is] rich, [with] large black walnut timber. We pass some large improvements and go some distance on the bluffs (crossing some branches) before we come into Fishing River bottom. We ford [the] Fishing which is about belly-deep on our horses, [and] mostly back water (it being but [a] small creek). There is an old Indian encampment on the east bank of [the] Fishing River, as well as at several other places we passed today. The bottom immediately on the west bank of Fishing River is very wet and swampy as we continued partly up it a mile or two; on leaving the swamp, however, we enter high, dry, rich land, lying nearly level and covered with large sugar trees. It appears to be as rich and black [a] soil as I have ever seen. One Captain Parmer has settled near this and intends (I understand) buying it at the sale. This is of no great extent, and we soon descend a steep bank into the Missouri bottom, which has nothing peculiarily to distinguish it from the other good bottoms. (One thing I forgot to mention is that the swamp of [the] Fishing River is the worst infested with musketoes [sic] of any I have ever been in.) After continuing along the bottoms some time, we enter what the inhabitants call a slew or sluice; it has no water in it now and is extremely rich. Between it and the river there is a tolerable extensive prairie reaching not quite to the river; it is in the first bottom, the sluice running along the bank of the second, in which the road continues (I suppose) 1½ miles; we then enter the timber, presently leave the bottom, and pass through some broken, thin land for 2 or 3 miles. We arrive at one James's encampment and improvement where the land is rich and lays well. Here we encamp being something upwards of 20 miles from Bluffton.

7th (Wednesday) The lands we pass through this morning are generally good, with some exceptions mostly first rate. In about 5 miles we reach Rush Creek where there is a considerable settlement and large improvements for the time; last winter there was not a white family this far up. Here the land is nearly all good and continues pretty much the same as high up as we have been, which was on Little Blue Creek, and within about 6 miles of the boundary line (Range 32). The face of the country is not entirely level, and yet it cannot be called "hilly." It swells into gentle rises and undulating plains, intersected by little streams of running water which flow from the purest fountains; and, as for the soil, it exceeds in appearance anything I have ever seen for richness. It is as black and (where it has been recently plowed) not unlike in appearance to gunpowder. The[re are] black walnut and pin-oak, which are allowed to be the richest growth of this country; on the whole, considering the richness of the soil, the goodness of the timber, the abundance of good and wholesome water, the favorable situation of the land, the luxurious profusion of the grass and weeds which cover it and which is the most delightful range for stock, I don't know a new country that could offer greater inducements to the settler. With a comparatively small portion of labor, he can convert a part of the forest into productive fields, as it requires little else to clear it than just to deaden the timber and fence in as much as he can attend; there is scarce any undergrowth, excepting chance places, and consequently requires no grubbing. The ease of making a farm may be easily perceived by the extensive ones that have been made mostly in the course of a few months. Owing to our short stay in this part, we could take but a very superficial survey of the country, but if I may judge from what I have seen and from the best information I could collect, I should not hesitate in pronouncing it the best part of the Missouri. I have been told that there are good seats for water mills, if not in abundance, in many places through the country, which is an additional inducement to settlers. From [the] Little Blue to the boundary line, and even above, I am told the country is nothing inferior to that which I have attempted to describe. From our own observation we could form but a very imperfect idea of the bounds or quantity of good land, but from the best information we could collect, the breadth of timber from the river to the Grand Prairie is about 40 miles. We have made a retrograde movement this evening, and have put up for the night at a Mr. Richie's, with whom I had some former acquaintance.

8th (Thursday) We cross Rush Creek this morning and continue our course toward home; we pass through Bluffton about 12 and arrive at Turner's late in the evening, having passed an improvement in [the] prairie which shows how little timber will serve for the settlement of prairies. There is about 40 acres by a small ditch and [a] fence made of sod which is tough and has been cut in straight pieces and laid up with almost the same regularity as brick; the grass on the sods is a-growing and unites them together, which will make a firm and durable fence.

9th (Friday) Leave Turner's about 9 o'clock, cross skirt of the prairie to Crooked River, about 3 miles, where we ferry ourselves over; the weather is extremely hot and sultry; some appearance of rain but, not withstanding, we enter the big prairie through which it is 30 miles to the runt house. We had not proceeded more than 8 miles, and were near the Round Grove, when it began to rain on us; we had left the track through the prairie to go by the Round Grove. The timber in it is tolerable thick but on account of the electric cloud that was hanging over us, from which the lightning almost continuously flashed, we thought it imprudent to enter the Grove and kept out in the prairie. We had no track now to guide us, but took the course as near as we can. The rain now poured down in such torrents that we could not see more than 100 yards around us. We soon lost sight of the Round Grove (which we knew was but a short distance in our rear), [and had] nothing now to guide us. [We] begin to be fearful that we might have taken a wrong course— and should it be towards the NW would lead us into the Grand Prairie (of which this is part) before we could reach any settlement. The wind now blew with great violence and beat the rain in our faces; the thunder rolled with an awful suddenness around us, sometimes bursting just over our heads in such dreadful peals that the earth trembled with dread; the lightning flashed so frequently that we were continually enveloped in the blaze which presented an awful contrast to the gloomy darkness that hung around us. It appeared as if the cloud, being surcharged with weight, had come down, was resting on the plain and then discharging itself in torrents. The awful peals of thunder, the violence of the wind driving the torrents of rain before it, [and] the continued blaze and horrible glare of the lightning, altogether presented a scene so terrible that it seemed as if the elements were at war with each other or were combined and raging with dreadful fury—just ready to destroy us. In all this rage and elemental war, who but would reflect how terrible is God when he clothes himself in the majesty of his power, when He puts on his terror, or frowns in anger? From the hollow of his hand He lets loose the thunder and from his eyes flash the dread lightning—who but would look beyond the effect to the more terrible cause? Or who would wish to provoke the anger of Him, who when he speaks in thunder, puts on not half his terrors? I am not naturally afraid of thunder; it generally awakens emotions sublime and pleasing, but I must confess that those awakened by this storm were rather more awful. It continued with unabating violence for many hours; we kept on the one course as near as we could. We had nothing to direct [us], [and] we could not discern a tree. All around us the extended plain was covered with clouds and thick darkness. The plain is so level the rain drains off it but slowly and our horses had literally to wade the prairie. The storm, a little abating, and the clouds rising from off the plain, we can see at some distance around us; on ascending a small eminence, we look out for the timber as eagerly as ever the tempest-beaten mariner, who, long absent from land, looked out for it when he expected he was near; and soon after we discovered, at a great distance before us, the West Grove, and soon after the Round Grove [was] behind us and we [were] nearly in a line between the two, which satisfy'd us that we were right. We hurried on then to cross the Waquenda before it should raise; on arriving at it, we found it considerably swelled. [We] expected to swim it but on entering find we can ford it. We cross the two forks of it and put up at one McGan's, supposing it to be near night; the sun breaking out soon after, however, we find it [is] several hours till night.

10th (Saturday) Clear and warm today. We leave the road through the prairie and keep down the bottom till near [the] Grande River with the intention of taking numbers in the Military bounty lands. It is difficult riding through the woods, the nettles very troublesome. When [we] reach the ferry on [the] Grande River, the wind is too high to cross, [and] we are detained several hours. It clouds up and is like for rain, notwithstanding which, and the lateness of the evening, we push on. It is 12 miles to the first house; we had not proceeded more than four when it began to rain pretty heavy on us; night was just at hand and was beginning to spread his dusky shades—we were afraid to cross Parmer's Creek in the dark and stopped on the edge of the prairie and turned out our horses. We seated ourselves on our saddles and reclined against the root of a tree; it rains on us for several hours; after clearing up, we sleep comfortable till day.

11th (Sunday) We start at dawn of day, [and] in about a mile or so reach [the] Parmer Branch where a family is encamped just moving up to Fishing River from Tennessee. We warm at their fire, then cross the branch (it is deep) and proceed on. The day [is] clear and warm. We reach Chariton about 7 o'clock; we wait in town till preaching is over, then go out to Mr. Burch's, and thence home late in the evening, having completed our tour in 10 days.

18th (Sunday) Go to preaching at Thomas Morris's; one Peter Woods preaches. Two persons [are] baptized, the first baptism I [have] seen.

24th (Saturday) The weather has been extremely warm all this week, the first excessive hot weather this season; today a very heavy shower of rain. I go to the singing school at Mr. Morris's. At night more rain.

25th (Sunday) Again go to the singing; [am] extremely low spirited. A slight cold.

26th (Monday) Clear and pleasant; [but] extremely melancholy.

27th (Tuesday) Go to [the] mill today and grind 7 bushels; pull flax.

28th (Wednesday) Finish working corn, have laid it by.

30th (Friday) Help Andrews reap. At night go to Susan's.

JULY 1820

1st (Saturday) Spend this day, as many others, in doing nothing. Sleeping or dozing away life. Not the happiest way to spend time.

2d (Sunday) Go to Mr. Meller's to preaching [by] one Mr. Buie. The evening I spend at Mr. Brooks.

3d (Monday) Began to rain early, before day light, and continued with short intermissions through the day—some hard showers.

4th (Tuesday) Still continues to rain a little, and has since yester-day—dark and gloomy; uncommon, for this country does seldom see more than a shower at once, and rarely a wet spell.

5th (Wednesday) Go to see Susan in the evening.

9th (Sunday) Go to camp meeting near Mr. Burch's.

10th (Monday) Go to Franklin to Court, [am] a witness for W. Andrews.

11th (Tuesday) Stay all day in town listening to H. Mitchel's trial.

12th (Wednesday) Start out early, a shower of rain after [I] get home.

16th (Sunday) Mr. Rogers preaches at T. Morris' where I attend—and from thence gather blackberrys with Susan.

17th (Monday) Help Buie hoe corn; extremely warm.

19th (Wednesday) Go to P. Woods' and buy 3 bushels corn.

22d (Saturday) Go to P. Woods' and grind [the corn]. Stay and see a shooting match there today.

23d (Sunday) Go to singing school at Morris', then to A's and H's and to _____—and disappoint a Mr. Ewing.

24th (Monday) Go to Woods' to work in his corn; he concludes not to employ us and we return home.

25th (Tuesday) Break a little flax, hunt berries.

26th (Wednesday) Go to Chariton. General Green, with a party of volunteers, has just started against the Indians (Quoys or Osage).

27th (Thursday) Go into the Missouri to swim; the first time.

28th (Friday) Beginning to rain this morning.

AUGUST 1820

6th (Sunday) Go to the Presbyterian camp meeting near Wear's, a very numerous congregation. Go home with Mr. Burch, [and] propose getting a school.

7th (Monday) Return to preaching; congregation not quite so numerous and more orderly and pious.

10th (Thursday) Go to Mr. Burch's and leave a school article, [and] from thence to Chariton. Extremely hot.

12th (Saturday) Shooting match at Bowers'. A fight [between] Burch and Jones.

13th (Sunday) Singing at Morris'.

14th (Monday) Meeting at Rooker's.

15th (Tuesday) Myself indisposed.

16th (Wednesday) Go Craig's Lick, hunt a horse.

17th (Thursday) Visit in the evening.

18th (Friday) Go to Holt's.

19th (Saturday) Cool and very like for rain, fall-like weather.

20th Sunday) Cloudy and gloomy, last night rain, today preaching at Morris's by Campbell and others; at night visit.

21st (Monday) Cloudy and gloomy, a little rain. Shoot with James Collins.

22d (Tuesday) Get ½ barrel salt from Andrews.

23d (Wednesday) Mother goes to Fall's with Miss Wasson; like for rain in the morning, evening clears off.

24th (Thursday) Clear and hot again.

25th (Friday) Rain, thunder and lightning.

26th (Saturday) Clear and pleasant, cool this morning. R. Wassons' shooting match.

27th (Sunday) Clear and pleasant. Last day of Fora's singing school, many there. I go to Susan Wasson's.

28th (Monday) Election [day]. I attend at Chariton; at night go to sales with Burch.

29th (Tuesday) Go back to Chariton; see a boat land there.

30th (Wednesday) Take wagon out, see Miss Susan home.

31st (Thursday) Haul logs for Andrews; at night [attend] Bennett's wedding.

SEPTEMBER 1820

1st (Friday) Rainy morning, then clear. Jacks raise a house. At night stay at Andrews'.

2d (Thursday) Very warm; haul logs for Andrews.

3d (Sunday) Clear and warm. Singing; at night go to Susan's.

4th (Monday) Spread flax; excessive warm.

5th (Tuesday) Take fodder, extremely warm.

6th (Wednesday) Cloudy, a little cool.

7th (Thursday) Warm; continue saving fodder. Late in the evening visit Susan.

8th (Friday) Go to mill; 1½ bushels corn.

10th (Sunday) Singing school. Write petition for Burch, go to Andrews' and in evening to Susan's; at night a heavy rain with lightning and thunder.

11th (Monday) Help Buie with his fodder.

12th (Tuesday) Cool morning, return home early.

14th (Thursday) Go to mill with 4 bushels corn, nobody there.

15th and 16th (Friday and Saturday) Take fodder.

17th (Sunday) Go to preaching to T. Morris' and home with Susan; return home.

18th (Monday) Cool, finish topping corn.

19th (Tuesday) Cool and windy.

20th (Wednesday) Hunt horses, can't find them.

21st (Thursday) [Hunt horses again], find them. Go [to] Shipman's and Gerage's. An eclipse of the moon.

22d (Friday) Clear and pleasant; run a line for Jacks. [Today is] the anniversary of our removal. Write a letter for Mrs. Holt.

23d (Saturday) Cloudy, gloomy morning, then clear. Philips moves.

24th (Sunday) Clear and pleasant, visit Susan.

26th (Tuesday) Go to Franklin, stay all night at Dr. Hubbard's.

27th (Wednesday) Come home by Boone's Lick.

28th (Thursday) Go to mill with 3 bushels corn.

29th (Friday) Set up corn, like for rain.

30th (Saturday) Clear, etc.

OCTOBER 1820

1st (Sunday) Go to J. Burch's.

2d (Monday) Haul for Andrews; clear.

3d (Tuesday) [Haul for Andrews again] cloudy.

4th (Wednesday) Reuben Wasson raises crib; Susan.

5th (Thursday) Wedding at Burch's, severe frost at night, the first that is severe.

6th (Friday) Return home, at night I stay at Brooks', Susan.

7th (Saturday) Muster at Bradley's, rain at night.

8th (Sunday) Clear and windy; [at] night [I] sit up with Barns.

9th (Monday) Nothing.

10th (Tuesday) Hunt; [brother] Tom kills a deer; sit up at night with Barns.

12th (Thursday) Go to Woods' mill with wheat, can't get to grind. Sit up at night.

13th (Friday) Again go to mill, grind 6 bushels wheat and 4 of corn; return with [them at] night. Rain and some snow, cold.

14th (Saturday) Cold frosty morning, clear. Run a line for R. Wasson; sit up with Barns.

15th (Sunday) In the evening visit Susan.

16th (Monday) Cloudy and gloomy, work at stable.

17th (Tuesday) Barns dies about 9 or 10 o'clock at night, I stay all night; Susan.

18th (Wednesday) Help Berry, then go to Buie's and to Barn's burial about dark.

19th (Thursday) Haul horse trough, clear etc.

20th (Friday) Clear—nothing.

21st (Saturday) Go a hunting on Sulphur, stop at Fords'.

22d (Sunday) Clear, preaching at Morris's, from thence Susan, late.

23d (Monday) Begin to pull corn.

24th (Tuesday) Help John Waldon raise.

25th (Wednesday) Pull corn.

26th (Thursday) Haul corn, 8 wagon loads.

27th (Friday) Husk corn.

28th (Saturday) Husk corn; at night Susan, am severe—somewhat. Cloudy.

29th (Sunday) Warm and pleasant; two wagons encamp at the end lane this morning. Myself somewhat dis[appointed? distraught?]. Go to Shipman's.

30th (Monday) Husk corn on stock.

31st (Tuesday) Haul fodder, at night go to Burch's.

NOVEMBER 1820

1st (Wednesday) Haul corn, 6 loads; windy, etc.

2d (Thursday) Husk; Vagen moving camp in lane.

3d (Friday) Make rails; put up husks etc; Susan.

4th (Saturday) Make boards for Buie; Susan.

5th (Sunday) Go to preaching at McCreary's.

6th (Monday) Haul boards for Buie.

7th (Tuesday) Hunt, etc; very windy. Help Brooks pull corn; Susan.

8th (Wednesday) Pull corn at home, cold.

9th (Thursday) Go to mill, grind 6 bushels, very cold.

10th (Friday) Snow.

11th (Saturday) Snows all day very fast; at night it has fallen to the depth of 8 or 10 inches.

12th (Sunday) Cloudy and gloomy, the snow hangs on the trees.

13th (Monday) Go to Morris's for cow.

14th (Tuesday) Clear, thaws; kill a deer.

15th (Wednesday) Warm; kill another deer; go to Morris's and bring cow home.

16th (Thursday) Brooks husks corn.

17th (Friday) Haul 6 loads corn.

18th (Saturday) Haul 2 loads and set Andrews' house.

19th (Sunday) Go to preaching at Morris's.

20th (Monday) Pull corn at Wasson's; go [to] preaching at Andrew's. Measure Brook's field.

21st (Tuesday) Pull corn.

22d (Wednesday) Haul 7 loads, 6 home.

23d (Thursday) Andrews' house raising; haul 2 loads; measure Stotts' field.

24th (Friday) Husk all day and finish; at night Brooks; Susan, etc. Like for snow.

25th (Saturday) A little rain, cool, dull; in the evening cold. Measure rent corn for Andrews; a little snow; extremely cold night.

26th (Sunday) Clear but cold, go [to] Brooks' this evening, he starts on the morrow.

28th (Tuesday) A little moderate; go to Kinney's for hogs, don't get them.

29th (Wednesday) Cloudy and cold, in the evening snows very fast, about a foot deep.

30th (Thursday) Clear and pleasant, all to snow. Go Kinney's and get sows.

DECEMBER 1820

1st (Friday) Clear and hunt wild hogs.

2d (Saturday) Cloudy and dull cold.

3d (Sunday) Cloudy and dull in the evening, some rain and sleet, moderate; Susan.

4th (Monday) Election in Chariton. Clear and cold.

5th (Tuesday) Woods mill, grind 10 bushels corn.

6th (Wednesday) Hunt hogs, thaws and warm.

7th (Thursday) Hunt hogs and deer, cold.

Across the Wide Missouri, by James Brown Campbell

8th (Friday) Cloudy and dull, nothing.

9th (Saturday) Preaching at Wasson's, cold. Disappointment, no preachers attend.

10th (Sunday) Clear and cold, at night moderate; Susan home.

11th (Monday) Hunt hogs by Tharp's and Ford's, warm.

12th (Tuesday) Moderate, shell corn, thaws.

13th (Wednesday) Go Wood's mill before daylight, grind 10 bushels corn, a little snow.

14th (Thursday) Cold, snows; alter my compass.

15th (Friday) Cloudy and very cold.

16th (Saturday) Hunt hogs by Tharp's and Waldon's.

17th (Sunday) Preaching at Tharp's; at night Susan.

20th (Wednesday) Go to Chariton with Burch's wagon.

21st (Thursday) Go into Chariton, get a kettle, $6.

22d (Friday) Moderate, go to Burch's for sow; Susan.

24th (Sunday) Cloudy, work question.

25th (Monday) Go Fleming's at night and home.

26th (Tuesday) Brooks here tonight.

27th (Wednesday) Frolic at R. Wasson's.

28th (Thursday) Melancholy.

29th (Friday) Help Burch with stable.

30th (Satuday) Help Burch; at night Susan.

31st (Sunday) Clear and pleasant.

III.

EIGHTEEN TWENTY-ONE

JANUARY 1821

1st (Monday) Clear, cold and moderate; Susan.

2d (Tuesday) Cloudy and cold.

3d (Wednesday) Burch kills hogs; clear and very cold; at night Susan.

4th (Thursday) Cloudy and very cold; spring froze; hair cut yesterday; Susan.

5th (Friday) Clear and cold; ball at Sears'.

6th (Saturday) A little moderate; mend my shoes.

7th (Sunday) Clear and pleasant; snowed, frost.

8th (Monday) Burch takes mare and colt home.

9th (Tuesday) Cloudy and dull; thaws a little.

10th, 11th, and 12th (Wednesday, Thursday, and Friday) Thaws a little.

13th (Saturday) Rain and thaws.

14th (Sunday) Cold, cloudy, freezing; the roads very icy. Start to Bird's to a preaching; at night cold; Susan.

15th (Monday) Cold and slippery.

16th (Tuesday) Snow covers up the ice; hunt Fly; go to Perry's and Tom Wasson's.

17th (Wednesday) Clear and cold; the late snow about 8 or 10 inches deep.

18th (Thursday) Cloudy and cold.

19th (Friday) More moderate and snowing.

20th (Saturday) Cold.

21st (Sunday) Clear and cold.

22d (Monday) Cloudy and cold; borrow last; Burrass here.

23d (Tuesday) Cold, clear; excessive cold [at] night.

24th (Wednesday) Clear and cold; survey for Weer's.

25th (Thursday) Return home, clear but cold.

26th (Friday) Not so cold.

27th (Satuday) Moderate; thaws today, the first this month.

28th (Sunday) Quite warm and pleasant; thaws. Go to preaching at Miller's, clear.

29th (Monday) Cloudy and gloomy, [but] quite warm and thawing, the ground covered with water. I go to Chariton and Burrass'.

30th (Tuesday) Warm and thawing, the roads icy; return home through Chariton in the evening. At night much rain carried off the snow, nearly all.

31st (Wednesday) Cloudy and cool, the ground very muddy; go to Perry's.

FEBRUARY 1821

1st (Thursday) Warm and thawing; haul fodder; in evening a little rain.

2d (Friday) Continues warm, partly clear like for sugar weather. Try some trees but they do not run well.

4th (Sunday) Preaching at Bird's by Kavenaugh and others; in the evening a solitary ramble, disappointed.

5th (Monday) Write a letter to [cousin or uncle] John Campbell; go see Holt, etc.

6th (Tuesday) Go [to] Franklin and to Jorden's.

7th (Wednesday) Back to Franklin, then home.

8th (Thursday) Continues warm and muddy, thaws; read newspapers, dozen.

9th (Friday) Make sugar troughs; quite warm.

10th (Saturday) Go [to] horse race at Craig's; none return at night, muddy and rainy.

11th (Sunday) Rain and thunder in the morning; clears away and excessive high wind through the day; much timber blown down. Susan.

12th (Monday) Go to Chariton; get a letter from A. Lightner.

13th (Tuesday) Clear and pleasant, muddy.

14th (Wednesday) Go to R. Wasson, not at home. Clear, pleasant; Susan, late.

15th (Thursday) Go to Freeman's at Richmond.

16th (Friday) To Captain Owens', [then] to Bozarth's and to Robt. Morris'. Stay all night.

17th (Saturday) To Persinger's.

18th (Sunday) To Burns'; cloudy and dull.

19th (Monday) To Swearingen's school; at night to Purdenis'; cold, some snow.

20th (Tuesday) Clear and cool. Go to A. Johnson's to constable sale. Serve on jury before W. T. Carew, Esq. At night [go] home with John R. Swearingin. Cold and cloudy.

21st (Wednesday) Cold and cloudy; after getting a letter of recommendation from J. R. Swearingin to Judge Copeland, I set out thither. The weather turns extremely cold in the evening, [and] snows. I remain at Copeland's all night; he is a plain sensible man, possessed of genuine hospitality, divested of pride. I esteem him as a first character.

22d (Thursday) Snows, windy and blustery. I come up by Alecru's to Jorden's; arrive at night. Continues snowing. Too late by a day for any success.

23d (Friday) I go to Munro's and thence to Fall's, [and] stay all night. Extremely cold.

24th (Saturday) Clear and moderate; come to Becknel's and thence home in the evening.

25th (Sunday) Clear and pleasant, thaws. Sugar trees run water. Mr. Burch and his Lady here today, and Mr. Tom Morris.

26th (Monday) Very cold; go to Chariton, Court sitting; return late.

27th (Tuesday) Cloudy and cool; go [to] Burch's and Perry's.

28th (Wednesday) Cloudy, thaws; go [to] Chariton with Perry and Jones, [then] to Jackson's at night.

MARCH 1821

1st (Thursday) Return home early from Jackson's; go to sugar camp, trees run well.

2d (Friday) At sugar camp make 24 lbs.

3d (Saturday) All snow goes off today; at camp make 23 lbs. sugar today; at night [it] rains.

4th (Sunday) At camp make 22 lbs.; rain in evening.

5th (Monday) Cold; make sugar.

6th and 7th (Tuesday and Wednesday) Make sugar; cold.

8th (Thursday) Work on roads—and have a fight with R. Wasson.

9th (Friday) Return and work on roads; return home in evening.

10th (Saturday) Warm, at sugar camp.

11th (Sunday) Warm and pleasant; sugar trees run a little. A Mr. Carr here for books.

18th (Sunday) Cold, some snow on the ground; been making sugar last week. Go to J. Burch's in the evening.

19th (Monday) Cold; go [to] Franklin [in] pursuit [of] Wasson; return home late for witnesses.

20th (Tuesday) Return to Franklin. Cold. At night home; horse [goes] lame at Toolie's.

21st (Wednesday) Cool.

22d, 23d, and 24th (Thursday, Friday, and Saturday) Make sugar.

25th (Sunday) Cool. Mr. Carr here today. Make sugar; many at camps. Burch and Perry bring a letter from Wasson.

26th (Monday) Meet Wasson at Perry's.

27th (Tuesday) Go to Franklin; stay at Bingham's.

28th (Wednesday) Wait till late in Franklin to hear Gentry's trial, then go out to Drake's.

29th (Thursday) Return to Franklin and hear the evidence in Gentry's case. At night go out to Rawlin's with William Jackson.

30th (Friday) Return to Franklin about 10 o'clock; Strother pleading. Near night a jury brings in a verdict [of] not guilty. I go out to Hallet's in company with Paddy Woods and Burnam.

31st (Saturday) Start at dawn of day for home. A shower of rain, cloudy and dull, warm.

APRIL 1821

1st (Sunday) Go [to] preaching at Miller's.

2d (Monday) Cloudy; Jesse Jones here last night.

8th (Sunday) Go to preaching at school house near Rooker's and agree with W. Shields to lay out the town of Gallatin, Daviess County.

10th (Tuesday) Start up; go by Conway's and to Munroe's in [the] evening. Cold, with snow.

11th (Wednesday) Still snowing; a dreary prospect in [the] prairie. I go to Parmer's Creek and round its source, through [a] muddy bad road, and [on] to Grande River; Cameron there acrossing. Continues to snow; proceed towards the Waquenda, the track filled up with snow; find my way with difficulty. Reach Munker's late.

12th (Thursday) Overtake D. Gregg and Warren at Crowley's; accompany them through Big Prairie to C. Kiser Martin's. Clear and warm, the snow melts fast on [the] Waquenda, 16 inches deep.

13th (Friday) Reach Blufton at 12 o'clock, deliver my letters to J. Shields, [and] proceed with him after dinner to Parmer's.

14th (Saturday) After breakfast continue our route; stop at Hall's and then proceed to Thornton's.

15th (Sunday) View the site of Gallatin.

16th (Monday) Commence laying out lots. My horse goes to Brown's. I get Shield's and follow him; go back as far as Dean's and stay all night.

17th (Tuesday) Horses break out [again] early in the morning. I pursue them on foot several miles, [then] return to Gallatin without them. Lay out some lots.

18th (Wednesday) Draw map of Gallatin [while] Shields [goes in] pursuit of [the] horses.

19th (Thursday) Finish map.

20th (Friday) Go after saddle, [and] meet Shields returning (without our horses), bringing one for me to use. After dinner we go to Campbell's Groves and put up at Bond's; stay all night. Cold.

21st (Saturday) Go up [the] bottom by Atkin's [and] survey his land; go [to] Wilson's [and] stay all night.

22d (Sunday) Go by Melot's to Capron's and [on] to Harris' on [the] 18th Section. Stay all night.

23d (Monday) Return by Fowler's to Atkin's and to Richie's.

24th (Tuesday) Go to Estes' [on] Rush Creek, S. 5, survey his Quarter Section. At night [we go on] to James'.

25th (Wednesday) P. Parmer's, Wills', [and] I. Turner's; run his ½ Quarter; go to Hitch's [and] survey his ½ Quarter.

26th (Thursday) Reach Bluffton against 12 o'clock; proceed on to Woods' near Chariton River.

27th (Friday) Try line for Martin; reach Munker's in evening.

28th (Saturday) Proceed to Grande River, [and] ferry myself over. Feed, go by Munro's, to Chariton in company with Munro, by Conway's, and home late in night.

29th (Sunday) Go [to] Conway's.

MAY 1821

2nd (Wednesday) Left home about 7 in the morning, reached _____ at 10 and crossed the river about 12 o'clock. Proceeded through Boonville to the _____ River and in consequence of one of our mules getting mired in crossing the creek, we encamp an hour before sunset and dry our baggage. _____ is 5 miles from Boonville.

3d (Thursday) [Several illegible lines.] We crossed some streams of water running along a pebbly channel. [In] 4 miles we cross Clear Creek of Saline; clear handsome creek, rocky channel and soon enter another small prairie 1½ miles wide; some handsome farms around it. From there to the Moniteau, the land [is] much broken and not rich, black oak timber. The bottom on [the] Moniteau [is] a considerable width and [has a] rich growth of buckeye and pawpaw. The creek appears like it would afford good seats for waterworks; it, like the rest, has a rocky channel. It is called 15 miles from here to Boonville. On [the] south side it is several miles to one Mr. Yoe's, the first house on the road, from which place it is 25 miles to Boonville. [Several more illegible lines.]

4th (Friday) Like for rain in the morning; begins to thunder and the appearance of a storm prevents us from starting on our way. It rains very heavy till near 12 o'clock. We then fix up and start, the road rough, mostly hilly land, and small white and black oak timber. We soon enter a kind of barren with but little growth except brush and some scrubby white oak, [and] a great quantity of white flint rock. We cross several fine streams of pure water, the most considerable of which is called Rock Creek, [a] branch of [the] Moniteau; [it] is closely confined in by naked, barren hills on each side, with but little or no bottom land in it; what is, is rich but cut to pieces with the freshets, then naked hills at [a] distance, with here and there little groves and thickets of underbrush, [which] resemble farms or cultivated spots in a wilderness. [The area] has a romantically-wild appearance, not disagreeable to the eyes of the weary traveler (only as he estimates the distance he has yet to go) as hill rises over hill, to late in the evening. We reach Hinsely's on the waters of the Moreau, and, on account of its storming, we do not pitch our tent but lay in the barn. Travelled 20 miles.

5th (Saturday) Partly clear, fine growing morning. Our route is through the same kind of country as yesterday, poor hilly land, very stony, small white and black oak timber. In 6 miles we pass 2 houses near together where the land is a little better-adapted to cultivation; for a short distance (6 miles) from thence to the ford of the Moreau [there is] little variety and no settlers. The Moreau is swollen with the late rains. We have to wade near waist-deep, through narrow bottoms of good land. On leaving, we enter the same kind of poor lands as before, till, near the forks of [the] road, there are some handsome flat lands, [and] good large black oak timber. [These] flats [are] not extensive [but revert to] poor land again. It is 6 miles from [the] Moreau to [the] forks of [the] road; from hence to Williams' ferry, it is 6 miles, and to Walker's, 1½. We go to Walker's on [the] Osage, 13 miles above its mouth, [and] 6 from [the] Missouri River on a direct line. The Osage is a considerable river; it is 334 yards wide at this place. The platform not being sufficient to carry us all at once, it is late before we all get over, and we encamp on the bank under the bluff on the south side. The course of the river here is nearly east and west; the road we traveled today is N of E; we are about 20 miles from Hinsely's, our last encampment. Hinsely's is nearly opposite to Ramsey's bluff on the north side of [the] Missouri River, 4 miles. Walker's is the first house on this side since morning. In the night it rained very heavy, with sharp thunder and lightning.

6th (Sunday) Rain for some time this morning; we lie late until the rain ceases; it is near 8 or 9 o'clock, [and] appears like it would clear off. We are getting breakfast and intend going to the Gasconade. After breakfast we pursue our journey, the road very wet and sloshy; we soon leave the Osage bottom and enter the highlands, poor rocky hills. In about 8 miles we arrive at a creek which we never heard of before, but afterwards find it to be the Merries; it is much swollen with last night's rain. Our Yankee wades in till we find it too deep for our mules to cross with the baggage. After trying it several places, we concluded to build a raft, [but] after we have it completed, it will not answer any purpose; the current is so strong we cannot work it over. It is now late and we pitch our tent on the bank of the creek in hopes it will fall against the morrow. One Malcomb, who is moving to the Mina Burton, encamps here too.

7th (Monday) It is [a] clear, fine morning; the creek [has] fallen a little. We borrow Malcomb's horse and pack part of [our] baggage over the creek on him. We load our mules, [and] I ride one of them over; we pursue [a] route through the same kind of broken country as before. In 2 miles we arrive at the forks of [a] road; it is 12 miles from here to Herol's ferry on the Gasconade, and 3 to William's on [the] Osage. We reach the Gasconade bottom about 2 miles above the ferry. The bottoms are narrow and not of the richest quality; [a] large portion of the timber is sugar trees. The Gasconade is 110 yards wide here, it is 40 miles by land to its junction with [the] Missouri and 60 to Piny Fork where pine is plenty and many saw mills are erected. The hills on [the] east side are steeper and more broken than on the other, [The] timber [is] small black oak. This is the tract of country that was formerly condemned by the surveyors as [not] being worth surveying; it is now, however, [being] surveyed. There is no land on it fit for cultivation, except on the little creeks, which is a thin soil, part stony. We encamp on [the] West Fork [of the] Third Creek or Clear Creek, 10 miles from [the] ferry on [the] Gasconade. A small settlement [has sprung up] along this creek. The rain that fell this evening has made the road muddy and bad; in [the] night, more rain. 24 miles.

Across the Wide Missouri, by James Brown Campbell

8th (Tuesday) [A] rainy, wet morning; we delay starting in [the] rain, [but] about 9 o'clock it appears like to clear off [and] we pack up and start, the road sloshy and bad [through] poor, gravelly hills as before. In 5 miles we arrive at the main branch of the creek where we lay last night. There is [but] one family settled on the road here (there are several lower down on the creek between here and its junction with [the] Gasconade). The road is rough for a few miles from here, along a main high ridge (the divide between [the] Gasconade and [the] Merrimac). [It is a] handsome little prairie, a mile or two in extent, [and] perfectly level, with thin soil [and] skirts of oak timber jutting into it. On leaving the prairie, the road is rocky and rough for some distance. It then leads along another long ridge, [through] thick growths of small oak sapplings; [the] road [is] tolerable good. This ridge reaches down to the Berbice Creek, near the fork. There is scarce any better [land] at this place, and what is [here], is cut to pieces by the creek, which at times overflows all the low ground. It [is] now considerably swollen, too much [so] to ford. We [wander] among the sloughs till dark, then pitch our tent on the point of a hill, in the forks of [the] creek, having gone back some distance out of the bottom (being apprehensive of [the] creek overflowing its banks, as it appears to be doing. It has risen about 5 feet today). Thunder and some severe rain after we encamp, and as we did not start early this morning, we walked tolerably hard to get here. I am somewhat tired and my feet [are] extremely painful, having blistered the soles of them several days since—and walking in the rain yesterday has made [them] very sore. Travelled 20 miles today and passed one house in the distance.

9th (Wednesday) Hot and sultry. In consequence of the creek being high we cannot proceed on our journey. There is a man by the name of Reed settled here, but, lest travelers should trouble him, he does not keep any canoe or anything to cross the creek when high. We are under the necessity of making a canoe, which we did in the following manner: we [found] a smooth-bark hickory which was clear of knots and limbs [and] about 18 or 20 inches in diameter, and cut it off about 20 feet long. We then split the bark along the top and peeled it all off together, being careful not to split or crack it; we then trimmed the rough bark of the ends for about a foot or 18 inches, [so] that it might be pliable and come together the better. By flattening two pieces of timber and binding the ends close together with hickory bark and then forcing the end of the canoe between them we brought it close together. [We] fastened the top of

[the] sticks together with bark, [in] the same manner as the lower end, by putting in pieces of timber to widen the bark in the middle, raised the ends which were close, and gave her pretty much the shape [of] a ship with [a] sharp head and stern; we calked the ends with tow and mud, [and] she did not leak a drop; we launched her about 12 o'clock and she floated, [although] somewhat difficult to steer. I cross the creek on it and have some trouble to get back; we carry our plunder over and swim [the] mules over. We proceed on about 8 miles and encamp on a small branch.

10th (Thursday) Start early, [and] in 2 miles cross the east fork of the Berbice; there is a family living here. [Their] nearest neighbor is Reed, on the Big Berbice, 10 miles distant. We here take a left hand road by a water mill (being nearer than the main road), the mill 5 miles distant; after passing which we take a wrong track that leads us too low down on the river. We then go up the bank of [the] river, a cedar cliff, 1½ miles, to a Mr. Hide's, where we get a canoe out [of] the river which has been turned over. The river is considerably raised and very rapid; it is about 70 or 80 yards wide. We take [the] canoe up some distance to ford and carry our plunder over [in] 2 loads. Have some difficulty to make [the] mules swim. We then proceed about 2 miles to the main [road] and encamp on a little creek.

11th (Friday) Start early, [and] after crossing [the] creek, take a high hill, very rocky and rough; young Mr. Hide, who helped us over the river yesterday, overtakes me in about 6 miles and is good enough to let me ride his horse (by paying him well for it)—an ease to my feet which are very sore. The land [is] rocky, poor hills; [we] discover some pine, [and] soon get among plenty of it. It is the black or pitch pine. Altogether it looks quite natural to me, [since it] much resembles the piny knobs of old Allegheny. The pine continues till near the Mina Burton (or Potosi) where we arrive before night. Potosi is the county seat of Washington; it has a handsome court house, a white-painted, frame building, with some handsome columns at the SW end. The other buildings [are] mostly along a little creek below [the] court house. There are some good wooden buildings, [and] there is a mill erected on the creek [at] one spot, with a 20 or 25 foot wheel which drives 2 pair [of] stones. There are a great many [miners] digging around about here for minerals; they sink [holes] from 3 to 20 feet generally before they reach the ore, [located] in veins of nearly pure metal which [extend at] times to the depth of 60 feet. The ore is hard and white and in

[the] smelting [process] will lose about 30%. The [miners here] get $20 per 1000 lbs.; mineral and lead at St. Genevieve is worth $5 Cwt. The land here is principally reserved by the United States [government], except [for] some Spanish concessions which have [been] confirmed, such as [the] town tract in R2E, T37N and 80 miles S. of St. Louis. We encamp in the edge of town, having come 28 miles today.

12th (Saturday) Squire Brinker accompanies us a few miles. He informs [us] there [are] great quantities of iron ore near this place which is very rich, He states that it will hammer without breaking (the truth of which I somewhat doubt). There are iron works lately established here which make about 200 or 300 pounds per day. He states that the iron is nearly equal to steel, that it can be tempered and will answer for edge tools. He states there is a hill or mountain where great quantities of nearly pure ore [can be found]. It is called Iron Mountain and is considered as a phenomenon; it is covered with pine timber. Iron at the works sells for 10 cents a pound by the thousand, 12½ by the 100 and 16 by single lb. The road is cut out from Potosi to the line of Washington County; we cross into St. Genevieve County and encamp near a Mr. Garritz, having come 20 miles through some good land, none however equal to Boone's Lick County. 20 miles today.

13th (Sunday) After leaving Garritz's we pass several houses for 3 or 4 miles; from thence to near St. Michael's; [for] 10 or 12 miles there are no inhabitants. We cross the Franceways [St. François], a creek 12 or 15 yards wide and about knee-deep as we wade—clear, pretty water, about the size of Big River, which we crossed yesterday 7 or 8 miles from Potosi. Big River is about the size [of] Jackson's River [in Virginia], above the mouth of Back Creek, with pine timber on it. I also observed the honeysuckle in full bloom, which is the first I have seen in this state. St. Michael's is a small village, [and] the county seat of St. Genevieve. 20 miles today. We reach here some time before night and meet with Mr. Shields and Conway who arrive the day before and were impatiently waiting for us. I write back from this place.

14th (Monday) We all start together, passing along a poor stony country thinly settled, [among] some pine timber, [and] a good saw mill. Travel 25 miles and encamp at somebody's house where there is an excellent spring of water.

15th (Tuesday) Cloudy and like for rain. Two of our mules are missing this morning which detains us; the hands are out hunting them. Soon find them and proceed about 5 or 6 miles to the St. François River. We go part way and cross the river where it is fordable. It is 40 or 50 yards wide, [a] clear and gravelly channel; from here the course of the river is southeast. From the mouth of this river the base line for the 5th principal meridian commences. I observed some cane in the bottom, the first I have seen. After crossing the river we proceed through a piny country with scarce any other kind of timber in places. We encamp on a small branch among the pines; 20 miles today. A family moving.

16th (Wednesday) Proceed through a poor country 6 miles to Big Black River which we ford, carrying [our] plunder in [the] canoe; it is about the size of the St. François; from there [we go to the] Little Black, [which] is poor and [has] few settlements. [The Little Black] is a small river, [edged] with cane which is now common. We encamp here at an old Indian encampment and scarce have our tent pitched before it begins to rain very hard. This place is near the line between the state [of] Missouri and [the] Territory of Arkansas; it is supposed when the line is run it will be to the south of this. 28 miles today.

17th (Thursday) Reach the Currant River late in evening; it is 100 or 150 yards wide at this place and is navigable for boats of considerable burden above here. There is a town by the name of Currington laid out at this point on the south side of the river. We encamp 3 miles south of the river in handsome oak land; we have bad water tonight. 20 miles.

18th (Friday) Pursue our route through good land for some distance, timber mostly small oak. [It is] 7 miles from the Currant to [the] first house of a settlement; feed at one Miller's, [and] reach the Paushee De Man about 12 o'clock; it is a small river or creek about 10 or 15 yards wide, [with a] rapid and rocky channel. It is somewhat swollen and deep to ford. We cross in [our] canoe, [and] pass [the] new muster ground. About 1 mile from [the] river [we] take [the] right hand and leave the Davidsonville road. From here it is 10 miles through hilly broken country to [the] next settlement, the Widow Black's, at Eleven Point River. The river is 70 or 80 yards wide here, 10 miles above Davidsonville, where it unites with the Black River; we proceed 2 miles from [the] river and encamp. 22 miles.

19th (Saturday) Start early; it is 10 miles from Eleven Point River to the first settlement [at] Spring River; the land [is] mostly too poor [here] for agricultural purposes. We ford the river in [the] canoe (about 3 or 4 feet deep and 50 or 60 yards wide). Tarry here at a Mr. Hind's to grind our corn, then proceed by his mill, 20 or 25 foot wheel, [with] double gear. Meal [is] 2/bushel, [and] whiskey 50 cents a gallon by [the] barrel. From here it is 6 miles through barrens to Col. Stewart's on the Davidsonville road; pass Stewart's sawmill on [a] handsome little creek. It is 4 miles to [the] next house through good land, some barrens, part timber, open woods, small black oak timber. Limestone rock [is visible] near the surface of the ground [but] some places [are] naked. The land here, as farther back, somewhat resembles the lands in the Virginia Valley. Night [brings] some rain.

20th (Sunday) A rainy morning. Mr. Shields starts early to overtake Conway, who went by Davidsonville and has got [there] before us; we delay starting on account of [the] rain and cannot find all our horses. It is 2 o'clock before we find all our horses, then proceed on 5 miles to Strawberry River which is about the size of B[lack?] River; 20 or 30 yards wide, about belly deep to our horses, [with] large rocks in [the] channel. This, and all the waters we have crossed south of the St. François, unite near Davidsonville and take the name of Black River; it empties into White River and White River into the Mississippi, 18 miles above the mouth of the Arkansas. After crossing Strawberry River, we pass Jeffrey's, then enter poor barren hills covered with black jack, whortleberry bushes and some chestnut. We reach water about dark and encamp—16 miles today.

21st (Monday) Cloudy and like for rain. We start early, [and] in 10 miles reach a settlement. From thence it is 12 to [the] next, and 7 more to Widow Musick's mill. Here we encamp, 28 miles today. The mill is erected on a spring branch within ½ mile of its source, ½ mile from White River.

22d (Tuesday) Proceed 7 or 8 miles to one Harver's and camp waiting for Conway, who has gone to see a surveyor to know where his work commences.

23d (Wednesday) Mr. Conway has not yet come up; we are waiting for him. Some rain today. Conway returns in [the] evening.

24th (Thursday) We delay starting this morning, waiting to get Harver to go with us to show us the corner. I write a letter to brother Thomas. About 2 or 3 o'clock we start; pass through some tremendous hills and reach the corner from which our work commences. In [the] evening we encamp on a small creek.

25th (Friday) Cloudy and [a] little rain in [the] morning. On examining the corner we find we are 6 miles east of the right one. We adjust our compasses and follow the T line west over some very steep rocky hills, cedar and some pine timber. We reach the right corner in [the] afternoon and run R line south to [the] river, near a mile, and S line west over a stupendous cedar cliff and then [a] cane bottom to [the] White River—near a mile. This [is the] first work we have done. We then retrace [our] line 1½ miles, meet [our] packs, and encamp on a little creek with high hills on each side, cedar cliffs.

26th (Saturday) We start up the creek north 6 miles to another T corner 3½ miles; encamp in handsome woods, [but the] water [is] not good.

27th (Sunday) Commence work early; cross Rocky Bayou, at 50 or 60 lks. wire; run 5 miles over some bad cliffs.

28th (Monday) Continued my work; run a line down the cliffs of Rocky Bayou 4 miles today and do not reach camp till some time in [the] night.

29th (Tuesday) Carry out tier down to [the] river and return up Rocky Bayou to [our] camp in [the] night. Cross [the] creek eleven times [today].

30th (Wednesday) Commence another T corner, T 16 N, R 9 W. Run 5 miles today.

31st (Thursday) Run down to White River 3 miles and stay all night at a Col. Lynn's.

JUNE 1821

1st (Friday) Cloudy and like for rain; we finish our E mile, get tally points made, and return to camp.

2d (Saturday) Run down to White River 6 miles and lay on Rocky Bayou.

3d (Sunday) Run down to White River 3 miles and return to camp.

4th (Monday) Moved camp. Run in T 16 N, R 9 W. 7 miles today.

5th (Tuesday) Carry up D tier 5 miles today.

7th (Thursday) 6 miles today.

8th (Friday) Run 5½ miles.

9th (Saturday) Finished D tier, 5 miles.

10th (Sunday) Moved camp into T 17 N, R 9 W. Extreme warm weather, the first there has been. Excessive warm. Run 2 miles today. Gates [is] sick.

11th (Monday) Warm. Carry 1st tier in barrens 6 miles today.

12th (Tuesday) Rest today; Conway returns with bear [and] bacon; [he] concludes to start home. I write [a] letter.

13th (Wednesday) Run 5 miles to camp.

14th (Thursday) Work in D tier, 5 miles.

15th (Friday) Carry up middle tier; camp moved to [the] middle of [the] township. 5½ miles today.

16th (Saturday) Work on D tier, 5 miles today.

17th (Sunday) Work in 4th tier, 4½ miles up to standard line; Grimes takes a space.

18th (Monday) Go to northeast corner of T, run 3 miles.

19th (Tuesday) Shields [is] sick; I finish T, run 2½ miles.

20th (Wednesday) Move camp into T 16 N, R 10 W. I go with Shields to Darnell's in the N T end of Sec 12, T 10, R 9 W.

21st (Thursday) A cloudy, wet morning. I return to camp, work on T line 4 miles today. P.M. clear and warm.

22d (Friday) Continued T line over some rocky mountains, 2 3/4 miles to White River, then run a mile North.

23d (Saturday) Clear and warm. Waiting in the woods for hands, writing this by night. Extremely warm. Go to corner and meet hands. Run 2½ miles.

24th (Sunday) Moses leaves us. Gough goes out, run 4½ miles today.

25th (Monday) Move camp into T 15 N, R [11?] W. Kill [a] deer, nothing more. Very like for rain this evening. Mr. Gillet arrived at our camp last night.

26th (Tuesday) Heavy rain all day; don't go out of camp.

27th (Wednesday) Clear. We commence work early; bring down a tier to White River at French's, at the mouth of Sisler Creek. 5 miles today.

28th (Thursday) Rains heavy about 12 o'clock; get all wet. Run 2 miles and quit.

29th (Friday) Move camp to Martin's, run 5 miles. More rain.

30th (Saturday) Heavy rain last night and this morning. P.M. [is] clear. Run a line through Martin's field, 3/4 mile to White River.

JULY 1821

1st (Sunday) Clear, pleasant morning. Run a line along [the] White River bluffs; climb a stupendous cliff, 300 or 400 feet high, [and] have a handsome vision of White River. Comes up a thunder storm and heavy rain, after which we continue work, 3 miles today. Returning home I fall on a slippery rock and nearly ruin my compass.

2d (Monday) Clear morning; run 3 [miles] west to Chandler's and White River, where [I] stay all night. Run 4 miles today.

3d (Tuesday) Run a line from Chandler's down White River through the thick cane which was wet by the rain last night; get all wet. Get breakfast at Chandler's, [and] meet other company. Run 3 miles; showery and disagreeable. Clothes wet, [I] return to camp; everything wet.

4th (Wednesday) Move camp; cloudy and like for rain. Meet with Shields at Pelham's, [and] run about 4 miles through Jeffrey's cornfield and encamp before night. Go into White River to swim, get a drink of whisky—and so finish the celebration of the birthday of American Independence.

5th (Thursday) Clear pleasant morning; our mules missing, [so] we are late starting; very warm. We reach our work (9 miles distant) about 12 o'clock, run 4 miles and encamp on a little creek between high hills.

6th (Friday) A cloudy morning; we start early, cross the Piny Bayou and some whortleberry ridges, thence to White River. 4 miles today, [and] finish before night.

7th (Saturday) A rainy morning. Go out to work, get wet, run 2 miles and quit. Gates sick, myself not very well. In the evening [I] go to correct an East random line between Sec. 15 and 22. I am now in the woods alone writing this, Congo feeding round me. The weather cloudy and gloomy, like for rain. I cast a thought towards home, [and] look forward for happier days when, far distant from here, I may read this, [and] reflect where once I was. How vain [is] the thought that I should see those days of felicity, when I can review my past life with any degree of pleasure, [and] retrace (as in a map) the voyager, his course, [and] the wanderings of his ways through many years. But it is the nature of man to lay up happiness for the future. He never enjoys the present moment, but ponders on the past or future— both beyond his reach. Yet I enjoy the present moment although I am wet and cold—and so I start to correct my line.

8th (Sunday) Start out early to work; cross one branch [of] the Piny Bayou running north. Begins to rain. Running south cross the Piny Bayou below the fork. [It is] a considerable creek, 2 lks. wide and about waist deep to us as we wade it. The cliffs on the north side make a very grand and sublime appearance; they are composed of a hard, flinty rock and rise to 200 or 300 feet high in places, nearly perpendicular. At a distance [they] appear perfectly smooth, [and] resemble a vast stone wall. We clamber thro' crevices of rock and slip down trees to the foot. A sudden bend of the creek throws it again in our course in the same mile. On the one side as before there is a high cliff but on the opposite side of the creek, still however on the north. By this time [the] rains [are] very heavy. We are thoroughly wet but we stop under a projecting rock of the cliff and shelter till the rain abates a little, by which time we are chilled and shivering with the cold. We wade the creek about waist deep and continue our work. In the evening it clears up; in running east we touch a bend of the creek again and in running south to White River we corner in the mouth of Piny Bayou and return to camp by a little apple orchard and a fine blackberry patch. Partly dry again. We get 3½ miles today. Other company returns today.

9th (Monday) Warm; we move camp. Run ½ mile to [the] river, then run township line west to river 3/4 miles from T corner and commence meandering White River; run down in the water to finish corner and return to camp on the bank at one Jackson's. At night a storm of wind and rain. Some old trees fall around us, [the] rain beats through our tent, [and] wets everything.

10th (Tuesday) Get a perriogue [pirogue] and proceed on meandering down the river; it rose about 3 feet last night, much against us. We wade chiefly in the water, get about 3 miles and encamp on [the] bank; cloudy and like for rain. Dry our things, sup on fish, and make a bed of cane; spread our blankets and sleep sound and comfortable till day.

11th (Wednesday) Left the water [and] proceed on through the cane; left part of our wet plunder at a Mr. Ramsey's whilst. I discovered a small streak of black cloud rising up the river in the northwest; it was just above the horizon when first discovered; it advances slowly. One of our hands, a sailor named Stoto, said we should have a storm. He said he had frequently observed such clouds on the southern coast and near the West India Islands and were always certain forerunners of frequently dreadful hurricanes. I observed this [cloud] to advance or rise steadily till it was nearly over us, still getting more dark and gloomy. The foremost edge [was] a black streak, behind which the clouds were dark and rain-like. But not so black as the stripe which reached from east to west as far as we could see (which to me was novel and seemed awfully sublime and grand). Our sailor said it was a wind cloud; we could hear the wind roar at a distance and when the cloud had advanced nearly over us it commenced blowing very hard where we were. Soon after, began [a] rain which was driven by the wind and beat through Ramsey's house in which we had taken shelter. After the storm was over we continued on down to Jeffrey's, the hands all anxious to get whisky. We pitch our tent on the bank in the same place where it was a week ago; we are wet. Tonight [it] rains again all night. 3½ miles today.

12th (Thursday) Still raining this morning; about 10 o'clock it breaks away a little and we start on measuring along the bank in the cane by Pelham's and to Purtee's where we encamp. Still wet and muddy, the river rising very fast. Exchange our borrowed pirogue (which is rotten and crazy) for a larger and sound dry one with running line.

13th (Friday) Proceed on early, measuring partly on shore and partly along the water's edge, having measured 50 lks. The two chainmen set in our boat, one at each end; the foremost would touch a leaf or twig or something that the other would notice and when ever he came opposite to this he would cry out "Stick" or "Strike," then the other would again touch or mark something. In this way we worked on, sometimes on water and sometimes on shore. The river still rising and runs with a strong heavy current much against our water measurement and likewise against our land measurement. All the sand beaches are covered with water and [we] cannot get along under the bank [because it is] too deep to wade upon the bank, mostly thick cane break. We get 3½ miles and encamp on [the] banks, raining. We have some difficulty in [starting our] fire; it rains all night, though not heavy. Our tent shelters us and we lay comfortably on our bed of bushes and cane.

14th (Saturday) Still raining this morning; the river rose 4 or 5 feet last night and is now quite muddy; where it is low it is remarkably clear water and [a] gentle current [in] a smooth gravelly channel about 300 yards wide. For several days after it began to rain it did not much change its color; in consequence of the rain and bad situation of the river I thought most advisable to lay by today. It has rained without intermission till about 12 o'clock when [it] partly cleared. [It is] still cloudy, [with a] little rain, [and] no appearance of fair weather. A very unpleasant time.

15th (Sunday) A cloudy dark morning; the river rose about 5 or 6 feet more last night. I don't well know what to do; we cannot get along well with our business [here]. Neither can we push our boat up to our other work. I'll try to proceed. Go a mile through the wet cane [and] pass a corner without seeing it; it rains a little. Try the river again; measure on by Martin's and French's and encamp on the side of hill under a cliff of rocks

200 or 300 feet high; cut away the cane and lay it in the lower part of [the] tent to level our bed.

16th (Monday) [The] sun breaks out through the clouds which is cheering after so long a dark wet spell. [I am in] hopes it will now be fair weather. [It is] very warm and sultry. The river has fallen a few inches, [since] last night [but is] still up over the most of our corners. Am plagued to find them. Have just returned from hunting one without finding it, [and] am discouraged. Everything works against us this trip. The hands are still out hunting, I waiting their return. The cane on the bank [is] immensely thick. The sun shines out faintly but very warm; [I hear] some thunder. Unable to find [my] corner, I proceed on to an immense cliff and establish a corner which was left when running [the] line. Could not get down [the] cliff; proceed, [but] can't find [the] next corner. The bottom [is] all flown [and I] can't get dry camping ground. I go on down the river, land on a drift heap and find a small spot of dry earth [where I] encamp near dark— more rain.

17th (Tuesday) A rainy morning. [I am] discouraged with our work and bad weather. [We are] nearly out of provisions. We fix up and put to sea again. [It] ceases to rain. We fortunately find a corner to sections 34 and 35. [We] continue on down and, after some difficulty, [find] our last corner under water. [We] start back with as much joy as if we were starting home. Find it very difficult working our boat up the river [which] has fallen a little. Return a mile and encamp under [a] bluff in thick cane on wet ground. Thinking of home and former times, a ray of peace comes casually across my mind.

18th (Wednesday) Clear fine morning, the first fair morning for some time. We set off early in high spirits for camp, make slow progress up the river; get along slowly. [It is] hard work. The river [is] rising [and we] cannot make any [head]way. Get about 5 or 6 miles and encamp at our old camp under the cliff where we lay last Sunday night. Discouraged about getting up [the] river.

19th (Thursday) Conclude to leave our craft; we start early and work her a mile up to French's (where we leave her and our plunder) and all set off cheerfully to walk to the other camp; have some difficulty in crossing the backwater. [We] reach Jeffrey's before 12 o'clock, get a drink of whiskey, some bread and milk and proceed on to Ramsey's where we left part of [our] clothes as we went down. I put on a clean shirt, the first for four or five weeks. We hear where the other company is encamped and put off again with alacrity; head [for] the backwater of the Piny Bayou and reach camp an hour before sunset where we meet our old companions with joy.

20th (Friday) Clear and very warm. We go 3 or 4 miles to work, survey 3½ miles in thick brush and return down the Piny Bayou to camp very fatigued; tonight it rains very heavy; we all, eleven in number, crowd in the tent.

21st (Saturday) Still raining this morning; we lay at camp all day, calculate Jeffery's fractional Section 30, T 16 N, R [11?].

22d (Sunday) Still raining, dark and gloomy, an unpleasant time to be in [the] woods; in [the] afternoon a very heavy rain. We do not go out [to] work but keep one Sabbath.

23d (Monday) A little rain in morning then clears off. I run the R line between R 10 and 11, T 17 N; run 7½ miles.

24th (Tuesday) The two companies separate. I remove camp up into T 11 N, R 11, which I am to survey at 50 cents per mile, and for all that I survey subsequent to this day I am to receive 50 cents per mile. I go along with the other company to adjust my compass to the standard, run one mile east on it, find it to agree exactly with it. [I] part with the company, [and] set off alone for my own company which are to meet me at T corner; after joining them I run the T line 1 mile west, then north and east a mile and close the old R line which I intersected in 72.00-400 lks. north of [the] corner. After hunting a long time I give up finding the line and set off to return and accidently discover it. [I] am at a loss to account for being so close. I return to camp without connecting the random.

25th (Wednesday) Go and run the 3 lines over I ran yesterday thinking I might have made some egregious error in running them but find them true. Then run the R line and in the first ½ mile fall 800 lks. east of [the] corner. The last half follows the line nearly. I then correct the east random and start up the 2d tier; run 8 miles today, a fine, level, open country. Jackson (whom I sent after provisions) returns at night sick and is unable to cook for us.

26th (Thursday) Jackson very sick; we get our own breakfast. Go out and run 8 miles, start up 3d tier.

27th (Friday) Start up 4th tier, run 7 miles, the weather fine, clear and cool, the country generally open and not very hilly. Was Jackson, our camp-keeper well, we could go on briskly. We have had to quit work before night to cook our victuals.

28th (Saturday) Remove camp today 2 miles north and 3 west. Jackson gets very sick while riding one of the mules. When we reach our camp ground he is so bad we do not like to leave him alone and do not go out to work this evening. Consequently [we] lose this day's work. He continues bad. I do not know well what to do. He appears to be too bad to leave alone. We are some distance, 7 or 8 miles, from any settlement I know of, [and] he is not able to get there. We cannot spare a hand to stay with him, having but 3 others, who [are] barely sufficient to carry on the work. I am in a very unpleasant situation. Thunder this evening and appears like for rain. I dread bad weather.

29th (Sunday) A clear fine morning. Jackson [is] still very bad. I do not well know how to manage. He is too bad to leave alone, [and] I conclude to try and send him into the settlement. I start (myself with Stoto) into the next township to hunt the other camp and acquaint Shields with my situation, [but] we do not know where to find them. We follow our lines east to [the] range line, then set off at random to hunt them. We pursue an east course as near as we can guess and fortunately find their camp without any difficulty, being in the center of the township 7 miles distant from our camp. We reach it about 12 o'clock and wait till evening for Shields to return out of the woods. I acquaint him with the situation of the township and also of my hands; he is much embarrassed about the situation of the township and partly concludes to go to the Lane's for instructions (which I oppose). He finally abandons that project—and as for the hands, he says I must go and hire others and shift for myself the best way I can.

30th (Monday) Clear pleasant morning. I set off to return to my own camp, dissatisfied at losing my time [during] this fine weather; reach home about 12 o'clock, having been fortunate in striking the lines, and meet the other boys who have just returned from taking Jackson into [the] settlement. We go out and run 4 miles. Nelson Witt [is] taken with a bad headache.

31st (Tuesday) Witt [is] still complaining of headache. I conclude to hunt a hand to hire; saddle up old Kate, a mule, with a pack saddle and start through the woods. It is about 7 miles south to the first house. I pursue my course, strike a path and reach Carpenter's about 10 o'clock where Jackson is laying sick—his sickness is now a confirmed fever and ague. The good people appear exceedingly hospitable. I take breakfast and pursue my journey, [on my] mount and packsaddle. I expect I make a respectable appearance to go to hire hands. [I] reach Martin's late in [the] evening where I expected to hire a hand. Old Martin himself [is] not very well, [but] concludes to send his son, a lad about 17 years of age, who I think will made a good hand. From thence I continue on to French's to know why he has not taken Trimble's boat home according to [our] agreement; reach there about sunset, my mule tired down and myself more tired than if I had walked—it is upwards of 20 miles from here to camp. I hobble my mule and turn her out in the cornfield and take up my lodging for the night. My bearskin and blanket which I brought with me are somewhat wet as in crossing the Piny Bayou my mule mired in the sand and wet them some. I was forced to dismount in the creek and wade out, it near waist deep. I lay in my wet clothes but lay comfortable and warm. I do not experience any bad effects from it.

AUGUST 1821

1st (Wednesday) I start early, pursue the road up the bank of White River about a mile to Martin's; [there is] thick fog in the bottom this morning which I am told is common and thought to be a carrier of sickness. Breakfast at Martin's on roasting ears and milk and set off with his son, Miles, to camp. The weather [is] very warm. Have a long parley with Trimble about paying him for bringing up his boat. He asks an unreasonable price which I am not willing to give. From thence I go to Jeffrey's, get a quart of whiskey for Jackson, and continue on to Carpenter's where I arrive an hour before sunset. Think it too late to reach camp before dark so conclude [to] stay all night. I feast on muskmelons, milk, bread and butter, etc; dainties to me.

2d (Thursday) Start early. Do not keep a good course but strike the eastern edge of the T, and follow the lines to camp where I arrive about 10 o'clock. Find Witt still sick and have yet but three hands fit for service; go out and run 4 miles, the heat extreme, even oppressive. It overcomes Gates who takes sick. [I] go on slowly.

3d   (Friday) Clear and warm. Gates goes out to work, [but] soon gets too sick to work—the heat excessive. I take the fore end of the chain myself and steer the compass too. Am in a bad situation again, my hands all sick but two and I know of none to hire.

4th   (Saturday) Witt's sickness now known to be what I apprehended, the fever and ague; Gates [also] too sick to work. I go out today with two hands, badly discouraged and a little apprehensive of sickness myself, altho' perfectly well now.

5th   (Sunday) The weather clear and excessive hot. I am discouraged with my situation, the hands sick. I cannot go on fast with the work with two hands, fatiguing on myself, too. I conclude to go and see Shields again not knowing but his company may be in [the] same situation and if they [want] to start one company out of the two. Me and Stoto again go in pursuit of them. Martin's boy [is] sick [now] and concludes to go home. We walk about 7 miles and find they have finished their T and gone off north into another, 6 miles distant. We return to our camp—young Martin gone and, tho' I have walked 14 miles today, I determine on going into the settlement (which is 6 or 7 miles off) this evening yet. I put on some clean clothes, my leather hunting shirt, and start with the intention of going tomorrow to an Election held at the mouth of the North fork of [the] White River. I go on to Livingston's Mill and stay there all night; lay on a feather bed, too soft for [me] to rest well on. It is 8 miles from here to the North Fork. I cannot borrow a horse, but am determined to walk there tomorrow.

6th   (Monday) Clear warm weather. After breakfast Mr. Livingston starts on to the Election and—very friendly—leaves me to take my time and walk after. I start on and meet Livingston returning to let me know that the man he [had] lent his horse to had another to take up and I could ride his. I then go on in company with him to [the] North fork, which is a considerable branch of [the] White River about 100 yards wide. We ford it and go on to one Adams' where the election is held. All the people in the country [are] collected here and [are] drinking whiskey very freely; they are truly a rough-looking set of people. I cannot make any engagement for hands till evening, then go ½ mile down river to a little store where the people soon collect to drink brandy and play cards—which they do nearly all night. I get into one corner of the house and cover up with bearskins where I lay till morning (after being frequently interrupted). They had respect enough for a stranger [though] not to proceed to violence in interrupting me.

7th (Tuesday) Set off early with one hand, having made an engagement with another to come out tomorrow. Yesterday evening and last night a heavy rain has cooled the air. I left the company still drinking and gambling there. About 12 o'clock [I] reach camp, having walked about 14 miles. I breakfasted partly on milk, etc. at Dyle's. Run 3 miles today and quit before night. Somewhat tired and am writing this by twilight in a little better spirits in hopes I can proceed with my work more briskly.

8th (Wednesday) A fine clear morning, pleasantly cool. Run 7 miles today; at night go down on North fork to one Woods, Esq., where I promised to meet the other hand that I engaged. I reach there about dark, cross Big Creek in a canoe, [and] find my hand waiting for me. Squire Woods entertains me hospitably and friendly; invites me to call on him again.

9th (Thursday) Start early, a fine clear morning, but the rain that fell last night has wet the bushes and made it unpleasant walking in [the] woods. I reach camp (about 6 miles off) about 8 o'clock; move camp and run 7 miles today.

10th (Friday) Clear, fine, cool morning. Start out early; [in] the woods which we go thro', the timber is thin and grass high; a very heavy dew fell last night and we get quite wet going out to work. I feel a little indisposed. [I] dread the ague but am in hopes that [it] is not. Think perhaps that getting wet yesterday morning and this morning is the cause. For some time past we have been in piny woods in which there is but little dew and I have not been wet for some days before. In the evening I am quite well.

11th (Saturday) Cloudy this morning, no dew last night. We run 4 miles today. Yesterday our camp-keeper Gates went for meat and did not return. We feared he was lost but when we return to camp about 3 o'clock he has returned and Gough with him.

12th (Sunday) Moved camp into T 18 N, R 12 W and run 7 miles today.

13th (Monday) Warm. Run 7½ miles. In perfect health. Nelson goes into settlement, Gates with him, and does not return.

14th (Tuesday) Moderately warm, run 7 miles.

15th (Wednesday) Indisposed. Run down to White River and to North fork, about 4 miles; stay all night at Zell's. Stoto goes off by himself to camp in a pit.

16th (Thursday) Stoto fails to meet us at the corner; we run into [the] river three-handed [for] 2 miles and go to camp. Stoto had sent Gates who could not find us.

17th (Friday) Yesterday evening there was a heavy shower of rain; the bushes are wet this morning, thunder and like for rain. About noon discover one of those dismal black clouds arising, portentous of a storm of which I have given a description while meandering the river. Moved camp today; we unpack the mules in a little glade on the side of a hill, pile up the plunder and wait for [the] storm. I cover with tent clothes but rain soon beats thro' it; it rains very heavy for an hour. When it ceases we continue work. Run 6 miles today and encamp near one Woods'.

18th (Saturday) The fog this morning is so thick and heavy that it obscures the sun and appears like a heavy rain was just coming on. It is near ten o'clock before it clears away; it is then warm. Run 2 or 3 miles on [the] river, [and] finish [the] township. [I] dine with Mr. Woods.

19th (Sunday) Clear and warm, move camp today into T 19 N, R 11 W. Run out T line 6 miles, correct it back with 3 miles and meet camp. Myself not very well. [I have] a bad taste in my mouth [and] spit a kind of froth, white and sticky, thought to proceed from a foul stomach.

20th (Monday) This morning, on going to wash myself, I find that we used nearly all the water that was in the hole where we have encamped and what remains is of a green sickly color. I do not like to use it, [but] make coffee. Move camp up into T today, run 5½ miles, mostly bad running, very brushy. In evening I feel rather worse, [and] resolve on taking medicine.

21st (Tuesday) Clear fine morning. I take a dose of tartar emetic, it pukes me but little; an hour afterwards I take a large dose of calomel and sallap [which] makes me extremely sick. [It] purges me smartly but little else than water through me. Too sick to stir about, cannot eat a bite all day, drink a little thin water gruel; at night sleep well but still very sick. Gates very attentive and good to me.

22d (Wednesday) Still extremely sick this morning. [I] begin to fear I am not to be well soon; drink a little coffee and feel a little better. Write a letter to Shields that I cannot go on with his business. Gates gets me some breakfast. I eat some and feel much better. Put on a clean shirt and take off a very dirty one which makes me feel [even] better. I post up my books today and in [the] evening feel well. Take some cream of tartar [which is] of service.

23d (Thursday) Go to run range line, walk 7 miles to begin, run 6 miles and encamp on Float Creek in a little grove of timber near a handsome little meadow thro' which the creek winds very pleasant; I feel somewhat tired but tolerable well, eat hearty.

24th (Friday) Return to camp, correct 3 miles on T line and run 3½ miles. [I] get to camp in the night, [and] find nobody there.

25th (Saturday) Go to work on 2d tier, cross Big Creek, run 3 miles. Gates gets sick, [and is] obliged to quit. I work on with 2 hands, run 2 miles more and return to camp in [the] night. [I] am agreeably surprised to find Mr. Shields there; he came with the expectation of finding me sick.

26th (Sunday) Quite well, eat heartily. Go to work on 3d tier. Mr. Shields takes the hind end of the chain, run 6 miles.

27th (Monday) While walking out to work this very clear morning, some of the boys observed it was going to rain. I perceived it was perfectly clear and that the sun shone faintly. Nature seemed to wear a melancholy aspect. I perceived the sun was eclipsed.

28th (Tuesday) Clear warm day; carry out 2d tier, cross Big Creek several times as I did yesterday. It does not afford much water but is some places 5 and 6 feet deep in holes, ¼ or ½ mile long and 100 or 200 yards wide; at a shoal or rapid it is not more [than] 6 or 8 yards wide and not knee deep. Our lines crossing it at some of these deep places, we are obliged to wade, which I have done when wet through with sweat without experiencing any injury therefrom.

29th (Wednesday) Carry up 4th tier and finish 3d, very warm. Squire Woods visits.

30th (Thursday) Some rain last night and this morning. We move camp from Big Creek to a fine spring, the bushes wet and disagreeable. I took brimstone and saltpeter last night and am apprehensive of danger in getting wet but go out to work on double tier. Get wet with bushes and wade Big Creek several times. Run 5 miles, more rain in evening. Squire Wood and Mr. Stinnet at our camp, Mr. Shields buys Stinnet's horse.

SEPTEMBER 1821

1st (Saturday) Cool, pleasant, and clear. Run 9 miles on D tier to-day, finish about sunset, 5 miles from camp.

2nd (Sunday) Finish Township 19, R 12 W. Run 3 miles in it and stay at Squire Woods' all night.

3d (Monday) Run several lines into the North fork of White River; clear and pleasant.

4th (Tuesday) Run T line between 20 and 19 T to river near Mr. Tobbert's and meander a mile or two. On returning to camp I am surprised to find Witt there and well of his ague.

5th (Wednesday) Mr. Shields leaves us and goes to the other company. Young Tobbert helps Witt, carries the chain a while and gives out; we run 6 miles, return to camp in night.

6th (Thursday) Run 2 miles and begin to meander from Martin's yard to 2 or 3 miles along the bank and return to camp in night.

7th (Friday) Finish last line in township and meander down to mouth of B. out at Squire Woods', mostly in the water.

8th (Saturday) Mules missing this morning. We go on and leave Witt to hunt them and come on to Hightower's; wade out in the river in places up to our arms; get to Hightower's about dark, no camp there. We are in an unpleasant situation, our clothes perfectly wet and no dry ones to put on. I however borrow a pair of pantaloons from Hightower, get some brandy and eat a hearty supper, after which I am extremely sick; puke several times which relieves me, sleep well at night but—

9th (Sunday) feel bad; get the good lady to make me some sage tea which helps me very much and start on meander, resolving however not to wade in [the] water. Go on down the bank [to] the mouth of North fork and finding it difficult getting along the bank of White River through the cane, I again take to the water and wade some places nearly up to my arms. Go 4 miles to our T corner and finish meandering near sun down. After I wring my clothes, we start on to Mr. Livingston's, 5 miles distant, [and] reach there an hour or so after dark. I had left orders for camp to come there, [but] it had not come.

10th (Monday) Witt comes this morning with the camp but [still] had not found the mules. The other company having come down as far as Woods', he got one of their mules and followed us. I am waiting here today for Shields to know whether we work any more or not, as the conclusion was when we parted that we would finish the work then on hand and go home. There is a letter of instructions here for him about surveying this township (17) but whether he will do it or not I do not yet know. [At] 3 o'clock Shields arrives, having found the mules. After perusing his letter and finding no money sent on to him as he expected, he resolves to quit work and leave this township. For, in fact, he could not well do it, being out of money and provisions nearly and several of the hands sick. Commence plotting the fractions in rivers.

11th (Tuesday) Continue plotting, examining our meanders. Rain prevents hands from coming to Livingston's mill-raising. He asked some to come today in expectation [that] our hands [could] help some. [They] come late and commence raising. Our other company which had gone yesterday to finish some work I had left undone, arrive in the evening thoroughly wet with the rain and assist in raising.

12th (Wednesday) Still raining very heavy this morning; the hands help raising [the] mill and after breakfast the St. Louis company sets off in [the] rain for home; the other waits. I continue examining meanders. Setting so constantly after such severe exercise does not agree with me but fatigues me worse than surveying. Ceases raining in evening.

13th (Thursday) Cloudy dull morning; the other company sets off for home this morning. They are now gone and [have] left me and Shields here alone. I could not see them all set off and leaving us behind without some little regret, altho' I expect to get along easier than if I had started with them. Shields has kept a mule for me to ride. I expect to be here a day or two and then overtake the company.

14th (Friday) Clear fine day. Livingston was about hiring Witt to work with him, [and] sent his son after him yesterday evening to tell him he would give his price, $15 per month, if he would return with him. The company went as far yesterday as Carpenter's, where Jackson has been ever since first taken sick. They start on from there this morning and Witt concludes to return to Livingston's and work all winter.

15th (Saturday) Clear and warm. We are still employed in examining our meanders. [I am] getting tired and impatient to get done, [and] sit up late at night.

16th (Sunday) Fine clear morning. We get nearly thro' with our examining and resolve to start a piece on our journey home. Settle our account with Livingston who charges us $3.50 per week for board, and about 3 o'clock [we] set off, bidding the country, as fast as we can leave it behind us (I think), an eternal farewell. We go on to Carpenter's, about 7 miles, and stay all night.

17th (Monday) Cloudy and a little rain, very like for wet weather; we anticipate bad weather to travel home in (it being near the autumnal equinox at which season it is common for it to rain). We remain at Carpenter's to complete our examinations and get the affidavit of Mr. Carpenter concerning the way a Mr. McCollom surveyed some lines on which we closed.

18th (Tuesday) Cloudy and gloomy, a little rain. We leave Carpenter's and go to measuring some lines in which there were mistakes. We ride 3 or 4 miles along the road, then pursue a line to the river bluff, hitch our horses and measure thro' a thick cane bottom to White River; the cane is wet and unpleasant. We then strike for the road and pursue it, crossing the Piny Bayou down below Pelham's, where we have another line to remeasure. We find an out missed on it, we establish a ½ mile corner and return up to Jeffrey's and remeasure the lines of fractional Section 19, [and] find another out miss which completes our rectifying [of] errors committed in surveying on the river; we put up at Squire Jeffrey's and with some degree of pleasure conclude our summer's work is over, and that tomorrow we will be on our way home and have nothing to detain us further.

19th (Wednesday) Mr. Shields swaps his horse for one of Jeffrey's, [which is] much better, and agrees to give him $20 to boot; he is a fine large noble animal and after breakfast we start on our journey, Shields in high spirits of soon reaching St. Louis on his fine horse. But fortune was against [us] and resolved to throw cross accidents in our way to retard our progress and detain us in this wretched country. We had not gone more then 4 or 5 miles when his horse was taken sick. We pushed on to the first house on [the] road, a Mr. Trimble's, about 15 miles from Jeffrey's, where the horse was badly swelled with the colick and, in spite of all we could do for him, soon died in the greatest agony and left us to foot our way home. Trimble is good enough to let us have a horse to ride a few miles, after which we pack our plunder on the mule and walk on; it is 14 miles to the next house. It is now late in afternoon, the day is very warm and the road rough. We walk very hard but are not able to reach Goin's (the first house) before dark. The road is but a dim track and it is very dark in the thick timber, which renders it difficult to follow the road. At length we finally lose it but are in hearing of some bells which we conclude are near some house. I "halloo" and am glad to hear an answer. We make toward the place from whence it came and after repeatedly hallooing and being answered, we reach a creek. After crossing, we reach the house and find one man [by] the name of Dunn living there by himself. He feeds our mule and entertains us hospitably on venison, bread and milk. We spread our blankets on the floor and sleep well till near day.

20th (Thursday) Start at dawn of day, recross the creek and in about ¼ or ½ mile pass Goin's, the place where we first encamped when we began to survey. The day is fine. We are now about to leave the country in which we have been so long. The contrast of the present with the last time I was here cannot but awaken some emotions not unpleasant. We were beginning then a summer's work; it is now ended and we [are] on our way home. We walk on about 8 miles to one Staten's, a place I also remember to have passed in the spring; it is in a level, pleasant valley, partly barrens, with small timber which has more the appearance of trees planted by hand than nature's works. It looks delightful to me, being a cultivated region. After breakfasting here we proceed on by Musick's Mill, one of our old encampments, to Batesville on Poke Bayou, and from thence to Boswell's at the town of Napoleon on the bank of [the] White River. Boswell lends Shields some money to bear our expenses home; in [the] evening we proceed on our journey and bid a final farewell to White River. We pass thro' a level handsome country about 12 miles to one St. Clair's, where we left the Poke Bayou road last spring. It is in the night when we reach here, [and] the lady is good enough not to let us stay. After some imparting we start on, [and] in about ½ mile come to another house where we stay, having travelled about 30 miles today.

21st (Friday) Cloudy and rain-like. We start early, pass two houses. From the last it is 15 miles to Jeffrey's, where [we] stop for breakfast. We then proceed across Strawberry River and, it appearing like for a shower of rain, we stop at one Taylor's, a distant connection of Shields; there is presently a heavy shower of rain. Mr. Shields is unwell, has a slight chill and fever; we conclude to remain here till the morrow and I make me a pair of moccasins. Col. John Miller of Davidsonville, whom I had seen yesterday at Poke Bayou, stays here tonight.

22d (Saturday) Mr. Shields some better this morning. We get the loan of a horse to ride to Col. Stewart's, 9 miles. We start early, pass another of our old encampments, [and] get to Stewart's for breakfast; it is a little cloudy and rain-like. We get a horse of Stewart to ride to the ferry, a mile above Davidsonville. The ferry is immediately below the junction of Spring River and Eleven Point, where the river is about 80 yards wide. It is a mile or so upwards from here to the junction with Black River just below Davidsonville, from which it is about 150 miles to its mouth at White River. Davidsonville is a neat little village, pleasantly situated in the fork of the river; it is the county seat for Lawrence; it has a good log jail and a brick court house is now building. Mr. Shields makes his situation known to a young Mr. Pelham, a surveyor who treats us very politely, and he is good enough to get a horse and lend him to [Shields to] ride to St. Louis. He invites us to dine with him at the tavern and will not let Shields pay a cent for it. After being both again mounted, we proceed on our journey in better spirits. We meet two travelers who inform us that John Shields is a few miles, 8 or 9, back, coming on to meet us. We then spur on to get to the place. About sunset [we] meet him, [and] he turns back with us and rides some time in [the] night to get to where he left his horse at one Capt. Glenn's, 15 miles from Davidsonville. Travelled in the whole about 35 miles today.

23d (Sunday) Clear and pleasant. We ride on good road to the Currant, 15 miles, where we stop at one Miller's for breakfast. Before it can be got ready Shields is taken with a chill and fever and cannot eat; he is not well enough to travel. I wait all day; this appears like a sickly place. The people are sick and look ill-like; it is about 12 miles from here to where the Currant discharges itself into Black River.

24th (Monday) Shields is better this morning but concludes to wait and take medicine. I fix up and after breakfast start on and leave him. Cross the Currant about 9 o'clock. It is about 8 yards wide and shallow enough now to pole. I proceed on alone about 27 miles and put up at one Proctor's in company with another old gentleman who is going to Jackson. Pay 2/3.

25th (Tuesday) Cloudy and like for rain. Start early, [and] it soon comes on rain; I put my blanket round me and ride on to Big Black River which I find lower than when I last crossed it. I ford it and stop at Bullenou's for breakfast, 12 miles from Proctor's. I wait an hour or two here—it ceases raining and I proceed on late in [the] afternoon. Cross the St. François at Dr. Bethers'; it is now but a creek not more than knee-deep at [the] ford. There is a small settlement here on the river and some distance down another small settlement, and from thence till near the Mississippi it is a wilderness. The St. François loses itself in the great swamp but recovers its channel about 80 miles before it empties into the Mississippi. After crossing I pass thro' the town of Greenville which is laid out in a handsome bottom. It is the county seat for Wayne County; it has but two or three houses as yet in it, [and] one is a tavern. I get a pint whiskey here and proceed 3 miles further where we turned off the road last spring to cross [the] river. At night I am sick with a bad dysentery. Here pay 3/9 for very little.

26th (Wednesday) This morning I do not feel well. I cut me some cane and start late. Proceed on to Shelton's, the place we first encamped last spring after leaving St. Michael's. I feed my mule here and wait for late dinner (my breakfast) then go [on] a new road 8 miles to one Mr. Campbell's and put up for the night. Pay 2/3 at Shelton's.

27th (Thursday) Start early. It is 12 miles from here to St. Michael's, [and] 9 to the first house. It begins to rain about the time I reach St. Michael's; from here I go to the French village and get a shoe removed on my mule. It [is] still raining. I then proceed on the St. Louis road 12 miles to a Mr. Somebody's and put up for the night. It rains incessantly. Three men arrive here in the night from the mines and wish to stay, [but] say they have no money. My host takes them in.

28th (Friday) Still raining very hard this morning. I wait till after breakfast; it slacks raining a little and I start on, pay 4/6. It begins to rain again and I put my blanket about me and ride on through the Murphy settlement. It is a handsome country, the soil a dark reddish color, produces well. There are some considerable improvements, large farms and good log buildings. I pass some fine apple orchards, it appears like the people live comfortable; the land is gently rolling and somewhat resembles the Kentucky lands. On Big River there is likewise a good settlement after which it is a poor stony country. I spur on to cross Big River before it rises, I cross an hour or so before night. Pass two houses and not knowing but what it was settled all along the road I push on. I ride some distance till night overtakes me anxiously looking for a house but can see no appearance of any improvements. It still rains, I am wet and hungry and do not wish to lay out which am fearful I shall. I climb hill after hill till sometime in [the] night with the hopes of seeing a cheerful blazing fire or the hand of man. It is too dark to see the road and I conclude to go down a hill and stop; when I get down I discover joyfully a distant light. I make towards it and find it proceeds from the house of one Spalding. I put up with him; he says it is 6 miles back [to] the last house I passed and 8 miles to Shibolah and 9 to Mina Burton.

29th (Saturday) I get some biscuit baked this morning at Spalding's and then start on late. Pass one or two houses, and then enter the valley of Potosi. I stop an hour or so here, get a quart of whiskey and proceed. On leaving town I take a wrong road and go several miles out of my way. After I get in the road again, I go to one Watson's 10 miles from Potosi, and from which it is 10 miles to next house on road. Soon after I stop there is a little ____. There has been lately discovered a bed of mineral near here and there are many hands working. A Mr. Smith from Franklin boards here.

30th (Sunday) Start at dawn of day, a little shower of rain and very gloomy; it however soon clears up and is a fine day. I cross those barren piny ridges which I crossed last May, stop at a waste house. I feed my mule, then pass one of our encampments and proceed to the Merrimack. The Merrimack is raised by the late rains and too deep to ford; I cross in [a] canoe and swim my mule along side. I then proceed about 12 or 14 miles over chiefly poor, stony, hilly land with some barrens to one Hide, who lives on the little Berbice and which is the first house on the road from [the] Merrimack. I stay here all night, have supper, pay 12½ cents.

OCTOBER 1821

1st (Monday) A fine, clean, cold morning. I start early, reach Reed's on the Big Berbice for breakfast. The Berbice has been very high but is falling; it is too deep to ride dry on my mule, and [I] borrow a horse of Reed to ride over, after which I find some of its branches deep enough to wet me. The road [is] somewhat sloppy and wet. About noon or a little after I reach the little prairie. It is delightful [and] appears more beautiful than what it did last spring. It was naked [then], the grass just starting in it; [now] it is covered with a rich profusion of grass as high as a man's shoulder; it is now perfectly level and [is] so different from most of country I [have] seen lately that it had truly a pleasing and delightful appearance. In the prairie I meet a family moving from Boone's Lick to Kentucky; they give a bad account about sickness. Soon after leaving [the] prairie [I] reach the poor stony hills of Third Creek, which I cross late in the afternoon. Pass the second Reed's and go over those stony hills which I walked last spring in so much pain to the first Reed's, where I put up in the poorest house I ever stayed at; but I made me a good fire, spread my blankets, and slept very comfortable till day. I then...

2d (Tuesday) proceed on to the Gasconade; it is likewise very high and the back water in the bottom is quite deep to ride; nearly swim [my] little mule. When I reach the Gasconade the boat is on the other side and the man who attends to her [is] gone from home. The rest of the family, 14 in number, are all sick. They exhibit a wretched picture of a sickly climate; they are not able to help themselves or one another, nor to obtain the necessaries of life for which they actually suffer. They have no bread only as they grate the meal, which for a sick person is no light task. Everything about them appears filthy and sickly. With these wretches I am forced to take up my lodging for this day; I assist them grating meal and at night an old Mr. Rainy from Tennessee puts up here.

3d (Wednesday) This morning after the boat is floored, we cross, pay 3/C [?] fare. [We] stop at one Berry's, an acquaintance of Rainy's, for breakfast, after which we pursue our route across some poor stony hills and fall over on to a little creek with handsome little bottoms; this road goes down to the Merries where there is one man settled. From here it is 5 miles to the Osage; the Merries is somewhat swollen but I ford it on my mule. It is mostly rough stony hills to Williams' ferry on [the] Osage where we arrive in [the] afternoon. It is 18 miles from the Gasconade ferry. The Osage here has a very majestic appearance; it appears to me like a little sea, tho' they say it is not more than ¼ mile wide. It is 6 miles from here to its junction with [the] Missouri (here R 10 W, T 43 N, Sec. 17). We are detained some time in crossing but have the pleasure of seeing a Mackinaw trading boat going up to the Indians. The Osage has but very narrow bottoms at this place, on leaving which the land is poor stony hills. It is too late to reach the first house on [the] road, 18 miles from Williams', and we conclude to turn [off] the road 2 miles to Walker's, where we stay. Walker treats us hospitable and charges me nothing.

4th (Thursday) After breakfast proceed on across the Moreau without any difficulty, and in 6 miles [meet] the two settlers mentioned in May. From thence we proceed to Hinsely's, one of my weary encampments last spring. There is a number of people collected here concerning a wolf hunt about which there is likely to be some disturbance. We stop here, feed; near here we got some of the most delicious summer grapes I [have] ever eaten. It is late in the afternoon when we proceed on, and [it] is 16 miles to Yoe's, [the] first house. We meet a family moving ([the] Packers). It is late in the night before we reach Yoe's. They are in bed; we get our horses put up and lay down and repose a few hours.

5th (Friday) Start early, pass a place where there has been digging for mineral without success. Soon cross the Moniteau; the country now begins to assume a different aspect from what it did when [we] last travelled the road in the spring. Now the yellow autumn has commenced his reign and the leaves are beginning to fall; the rustling in the trees excites rather a soothing melancholy sensation mixed with the idea of soon being at home and again seeing my dear relatives and friends after so long an absence. We proceed on thro' those beautiful little prairies mentioned in May, and in evening arrive at an acquaintance of Rainy's and get dinner, after which I part with Rainy; cross the Tête Saline and proceed on for Boonville. The whole face of [the] country appears changed; about sunset or a little before [I] reach Boonville and with pleasure again behold the Missouri. I ferry across it to Franklin and put up at Shane's tavern; hear my company had only crossed this morning.

6th (Saturday) Start at dawn of day, the roads wet from a heavy rain last night and this morning. Get a letter out of [the] Post Office from Henry Harold, then proceed on; about 8 miles [further I] meet Stephen Finell, who informs me the family are chiefly all sick, which very much damps the pleasure I was enjoying in anticipation of seeing them. Soon after [I] meet Sanford, who informs me that father and [brother] Thomas had gone in June last to Virginia, and had not returned. This was the first I had heard of their going and was more unpleasant news, as [I had] expected to see them all in a few hours. I then spur on past Monroe's, see James Finney and David Andrews, pass Tharp's, and in [the] afternoon get in sight of the house. It looks solitary; my heart palpitates. They soon discover me and a number of pale faces make their appearance. A fond mother meets me at the fence.

7th (Sunday) Remain all day at home.

8th (Monday) Go to Franklin to get medicine and necessaries for [the] family. Do not get home till in the night. It is cool. I feel a little unwell.

9th (Tuesday) Give medicine (tarter) to [brother] John; it operates severely. [I am] somewhat alarmed.

10th (Wednesday) Take a dose myself, it also operates very severely; am very sick till in the night, head aches bad. James Finney, David Andrews, and Nancy Wasson come and stay all night.

11th (Thursday) A little better myself but not well, feel stupid and bad.

12th (Friday) Same.

13th (Saturday) Began to shake about 1 o'clock, about 3 a very high fever to delirium; after it had subsided, a severe headache. I now had the shakes and fever every day; a severe headache for about a week when it left me, but the shakes and fever continued very bad.

[Suffering from a severe case of malaria, Campbell was forced to suspend his diary until the commencement of his family's return trip to their home in Virginia, in May of 1822.]

IV.

EIGHTEEN TWENTY-TWO

MAY 1822

21st (Tuesday) This day, about 10 o'clock, [we] left our temporary home, the place we first stopped at [on] the 21st [of] November 1819, and where we have ever since resided. A numerous company of neighbors assembled, some of them the evening before, to see us start on our long journey from the fertile Missouri to the land of our fathers. After taking leave of them, most of whom attended us on the road for several miles and several to our encampment, we proceeded on to the Bon Femme, which place we reached a short time before night, after having passed thro' Richmond in Spanish Needle Pass. It is about 10 or 12 miles from our residence on the head of Richland Creek, 6 miles from the town of Chariton, to our encampment on the Bon Femme.

22d (Wednesday) This morning early [we] took leave of our friends who stayed with us last night and proceed on [our] journey; fall into [the] Franklin road 4 miles at Salt Creek Bridge; from thence to Moniteau, 7 miles, where we stop and bail, then proceed to Thrall's, 4½ miles. From thence [we go] thro' the Persia town to Percee Creek, where we encamp about 20 or 24 miles from our last [encampment]. The Persia town is laid out on a hill on the west side of the creek; a number of buildings are begun, the most of which are going to decay before [being] finished. It exhibits not so much the decline of the country as [it does] an artful (or rather fraudulent) speculating scheme [accomplished] by imposing on the sanguine and credulous who purchased lots at a high price.

23d (Thursday) Cross the Roche Percee early, [and] proceed 2 miles to Grayham's where father leaves us to go by Brooks'; from thence [we] cross the rocky ford of [the] Percee, [and travel a] rough hilly road from thence to Hingston's, also [on] a fork of the Percee (tho' partly level and good). We rest at Hingston's then proceed across the 2 mile prairie by Estell's to Cedar Creek, one branch of which we cross and encamp on another near the west edge of the Grand Prairie near Gayhart. The distance we have travelled today is about 17 miles. Cool night.

24th (Friday) Start early, enter the Grand Prairie. [It is] unpleasantly cold this morning. We proceed across the Prairie 22 miles to Major Harrison's where we stop about 2 o'clock and feed, from thence proceed thro' timberland, rough and broken, to [the] Whetstone Branch at the edge of the Nine-Mile Prairie where we encamp. Pass one house, Ward's, 5 miles from Harrison's to Nine-Mile Prairie; the whole distance [is] 27 miles today.

25th (Saturday) Start after sunrise, [and] enter Nine-Mile Prairie. Pass two of the Fruits in [the] prairie, [and] meet with father there (he stayed all night at Fruit's). From thence [we] proceed to [the] Louter and feed, then pass several farms in Louter Prairie which is 22 miles long, narrow, and well adapted to cultivation. Before we get thro' a rain begins, which the wind drives in our faces, making it very unpleasant. We reach the Camp Branch at the east edge of [the] prairie a little before dark, all wet and cold. We cannot get any corn to feed our horses after driving them 36 miles today. One Ford lives here.

26th (Sunday) Still raining a little this morning, [so] we do not start till late. Cross a little prairie, then enter timber, [in a] hilly and broken land. [We travel] for 6 or 7 miles to a branch where we encamped when moving up (just above where we come into the road). From here [there] is another small prairie, then a skirt of timber and [more] small prairies, beautifully situated for cultivation. We stop at a Mr. Roundtree's farm in one of them and get corn [to] feed our teams. It is ten miles from here to Camp Branch where we lay last night. The weather [is] quite cold. We proceed on thro' small prairies and timber, pass Pringle's, a handsome Yankee settlement, then [on] to the west fork of [the] Barrack at one Scott's (who is from Monongahela, Virginia). The distance [is] 21 miles today.

27th (Monday) On driving up our horses this morning [we] find one amissing; hunt for him till we find he has taken the St. Charles road. We drive on 3 miles to another branch of the Barrack, to [a] waste house of Berry's. We encamp and turn out to hunt [the] horse. After some time me and Jones find his track and [I follow it] thro' the woods over on Dardan Creek, across [the creek] by McWater's, then to Chapin's on the post road, and

[on] to Rutherford. About dark I reach a house where I am told Jones has got the horse. I then inquire the way to camp, 3 or 4 miles distant, cross a small prairie, pass an old powder mill and reach camp sometime in [the] night.

28th (Tuesday) A fine clear morning. Pass one house and [after] some distance enter [the] prairie. Pass Bayley's at Pond Ford. He has a good house and [a] handsome farm; there is a pond back of the house from which the place took its name when the people forded there. From thence it is chiefly prairie with some handsome farms around them to a branch of (I suppose) the Dardan where we stop and feed. Then [we] proceed two or three miles, [on] partly wet, marshy road, to the Dardan. It is at present considerably swollen, [and] the banks are high and steep. There is a saw mill erected just above the ford. From here we pass several farms to Coon's, then proceed 5 or 7 miles over hilly, rough road to an old fellow's where we get some corn and meal. Here Mother misses her cloak and [brother] Samuel goes back to hunt it. We drive on to Sublet's on the hill above St. Charles and encamp. 27 miles today.

29th (Friday) Drive into St. Charles and from thence out into [the] Prairie which reaches from the Mississippi nearly to the Missouri. It is not more than 5 or 6 miles from St. Charles across to the Mississippi but wider. Below it is level and rich with many good farms in it. Part of the road very muddy and bad travelling; after a hard pull thro' a mud hole, Fox is very lame. We stop at one Piper's and feed, then leave [the] prairie. Fox is too lame to work; we stop at one Overall's to take him out and drive thro' his field, he gets in a great rage about tramping down his oats. We drive on to [the] next house and encamp, two or three miles from Smelser's ferry. We are in rather a bad situation, two of our horses are not fit for service and I do not know how we can proceed with the balance.

30th (Thursday) Start before breakfast; drive on to Smelser's ferry, 5 miles above the mouth of [the] Missouri on the Illinois side, and 6 [miles] on the Missouri. By the meanders of [the] river it is 6 miles below Port Ash or Portage de Sioux, and 14 miles to the mouth of [the] Illinois River. It is about 100 miles from here to the Sangamon [Illinois] settlement. It is near 12 o'clock before we all get over, having to make two loads. The river is something over a mile wide here. We stop and feed a short distance from [the] river at a good spring, then proceed about 3 miles to the town of Salie, [and] from thence to Milton 2 miles [further] where [the] road forks to go to the Fountain ferry. Alton, on that road, is not more than 2 miles distant, so that the three towns are but a few miles distant from each. Milton is on each side of Wood Creek; there are two mills, a saw and a grist mill, erected one on each side [of the] creek; there is a good wooden bridge over the creek. After leaving town we pass several farms along the edge of the bottom. [We] ascend the bluff, cross Indian Creek, and proceed on to a small branch in the woods, about 4 miles from Edwardsville, where we encamp the first night we have left Missouri, having travelled not more than 10 or 12 miles today.

31st (Friday) Our horses are missing this morning; it is late before they are found near the Coho or Cohokia, 2 or 3 miles off. It is very warm. We start on 2 or 3 miles, turn off to go [on] another road, [since] the bridge over the Coho has been taken off by a freshet; we are bothered some time to get into the right road, [and] it begins to rain before we reach the creek. We stop in a waste house till the rain is over, then put in 7 horses to go up a steep bank into Edwardsville; the town much improved since I was last in it. The sun is not more than half an hour high when we leave town. Pass some handsome farms in [a] prairie two or three miles from Edwardsville. Some very bad road, [with] deep "mirey" gulleys to Troy, which place we reach some time in [the] night and encamp. More rain tonight which makes the road wet and bad. Troy is in the edge of a prairie 3 miles west from Silver Creek. We have travelled not more than 12 miles today.

JUNE 1822

1st (Saturday) A cloudy, gloomy morning. It clears up, however, about 9 or 10 o'clock, and we proceed on to Silver Creek. Put in 6 horses to pull thro' a bad mud hole, [and] cross [the] creek on a frame bridge which has been erected since I [last] passed here. From thence the road is muddy [and] bad to the east fork of Silver Creek where we encamped when moving up. We [cross] on a good bridge, then enter [the] prairie, [where we] pass a company mustering [and] meet a family moving up to Salt River. Stop and feed in the Looking Glass Prairie, then proceed thro' it 10 miles to Sugar Creek where there is some bad road. Drive out in [the] prairie near Watkins' and encamp. Meet with one McFeaters here from Augusta in Virginia.

2d   (Sunday)   Start early, [and] drive thro' [the] prairie to Shoal Creek which we cross on a toll bridge (pay 75 cents), then proceed to Stinking Creek, 3 or 4 miles, which is also bridged. From thence it is 4 or 5 miles [through the] prairie to Carlisle, in the edge of [the] prairie on the Ocaw. The Ocaw is very high, [and] out of its banks. We ferry it (pay $2 ferriage), stop and feed, then proceed 2½ miles to one Lee's in the edge of [the] prairie and encamp having travelled about 20 miles today.

3d   (Monday)   Clear and pleasant. We start about 8 o'clock. Pass Adams' one mile from timber, [and] from thence to Huston's, [on] muddy, bad road. Huston's is 8 miles from Lee's, out in [the] prairie on an eminence which can be seen [from] a great distance. We stop here a short time, borrow a pair of gears and put in another horse to drive through a bad mud hole. [The] flies are very troublesome after leaving the prairie; they have been somewhat troublesome all morning, but much worse now. We drive about a mile and stop, take out our horses and run them back to the house [where we] kindle up fires to smoke off the flies. We remain here till about sunset, during which time I go and look at the muddy place in [the] road and search for a better way round it. We hitch in 6 horses and start on. It is dark by the time we reach the mud, but the moon is about full and the night nearly clear. I see tolerable well [enough] to drive; after hard pulling we get thro' the mud and [brother] Samuel goes back with the borrowed gears. I drive on with five horses. It is 12 miles from Huston's to Heck's, at a branch 2 miles into the Grand Prairie, [and] the first timber on the road. It is some time in the night before we encamp [in] one of our old camping places.

4th   (Tuesday) This morning (very early) it begins to rain very heavy; it continues raining till 9 or 10 o'clock when we fix up and start. The roads [are] full of water. We find some flies crossing the skirt of [a] prairie 2 miles to timber. There is a little creek a mile into another prairie 3 miles thro'. It is cloudy and cool, [and] the flies [are] not very bad. We then enter another slip of timber, [and] cross a creek, the Skillet Fork, twice. [We go over] some rough, hilly road, then enter a prairie 4 miles thro'. When we get thro' we are informed by some travelers [that] the Skillet Fork of the Little Wabash is swimming. We then stop at one Pile's [on the] edge of [a] prairie a mile from the creek and stay in his house as it is like for rain. 14 miles today.

5th   (Wednesday) Cloudy, sultry and hot. Some of [our] company go to the creek this morning and find it still high; about noon I go myself, cross in [a] canoe and try the depth—it is still high, 6 or 7 feet, tho' it is falling a little. I then return to camp and write this.

6th   (Thursday) Remain at Pile's till evening; see several travelers who have crossed [the] creek, among whom is a Mr. Davies and two ladies in a carriage from Chillicothe, Ohio going to the Vetecaw bottom, Missouri. The creek [is] high enough to run in their carriage. Late in [the] afternoon we hitch in and start; the weather [is] very warm. [We] cross a steep hill and go to [the] creek. After examining it minutely [we] conclude it is still high enough to run in [the] wagon bed and we encamp on the west bank at another of the Piles'; have travelled 1 mile today.

7th   (Friday) Start early this morning, [and], before breakfast, cross the creek, [which is] about (or near) belly deep to the horses; then [over] a muddy bottom for ¼ mile [on a] muddy road to [a] prairie 1 mile from [the] creek. Meet a hack with movers. The prairie is 3 miles thro', pass Murray's near the east edge at [the] forks of [a] road; one goes by Davis' and the other right by Fitch's across the skirt of timber from Murray's, 6 miles from our encampment. From thence [we cross] a prairie 1½ miles [long] and a skirt of timber, then another 3 miles [long] where the flies are bad. There is a farm on the edge of it, [and] from thence it is timber 2 miles to Eliot's in the west edge of the Twelve-Mile Prairie. Raccoon Creek, on which we camped when moving up, runs thro' timber. The flies are very bad [here]. We reach Eliot's about noon and stop and make smoke to keep the flies off the horses. We are waiting here till night [when] intend crossing the prairie. About sunset we start [and] have some very bad, muddy road, [with] hard pulling for some distance. We reach Elin River Creek in [the] middle of [the] prairie just as the moon is rising, 10 o'clock. 40 minutes from thence the road is not so bad to May's at the east edge of [the] prairie, where we arrive a short time before day and stay till morning. 25 miles.

8th   (Saturday) It is late this morning before we start; a family passes us going to Missouri. We drive down to McCawley's at [the] Little Wabash on a toll bridge (pay 75 cents). From here the road is very muddy and wet [for] 3 miles to the Muddy Fork, where [there] is another toll bridge (toll same here). We stop and rest till near sunset, then start on; in one mile [we] enter a prairie 6 miles across. The flies [are] troublesome, [and it is] very warm. It is moon-up when [we] reach Evans' where we encamp. Cannot get any feed for our horses, [and] have to turn them out. Come 12 miles.

9th (Sunday) Start early. The musketoes [sic] [are] extremely bad. Cross some timber and a little creek, then only stinking ponds. From there some muddy bottoms, then prairie and timber to Morehouse's, (7 miles from Evans') where [we] stop and feed. The weather [is] very warm. A heavy shower of rain [falls], after which we proceed; pass Delong's in a handsome little prairie. From thence it is chiefly poor, hilly land with some handsome, little prairies. [We proceed] to a little creek where [we] stop before night in consequence of one of our horses, Bony, being unwell. [Come] about 16 or 17 miles only today.

10th (Monday) Start early, the road good, chiefly [through] timber, and [the] weather very warm. We proceed on to Newel's, 7 or 8 miles, and stop to feed and breakfast. Thunder and like for rain. Proceed on 4 miles to Lawrenceville, a small village on the Embarras; from thence we have to go down the creek a mile to a ferry where we cross and swim the loose stock over. From thence we go one mile to Carn's and encamp, about 15 miles today.

11th (Tuesday) Start early, [and] drive about 4 miles through timber. [We] then enter the Ellison Prairie, which is level and beautiful. A great part of it is [under] cultivation. We stop at Squire ____ , near the middle of [a] prairie, from which place [we] can see 57 dwelling houses. The prairie (where it is settled) has large fields of cotton growing and some rice; [a] great part of it, however, is low and marshy, and surrounded by low, wet grounds which are overflowed when the Wabash is high. The settlement has been surrounded with water for several miles this season. We have some muddy, bad road in [the] prairie for about a mile. We then stop in [the] edge of timber and feed one mile from Vincennes. From here there is much water laying in the bottom to near [the] ferry. We cross over into Vincennes 2 or 3 hours before night and encamp in the prairie on the edge of town (pay $1.00 ferriage). [We] lay in provisions here, paying 6 cents for bacon and $2 Cwt for flour and sugar.

12th (Wednesday) It is late before we start this morning. A Mrs. Dunn has some thought of going with us. We drive out 8 miles to Snyder's and stop and feed; from thence [it is] 5 more [miles] to [the] edge of [the] White River bottom where we encamp on a hill. 13 miles.

13th (Thursday) Drive 2½ miles thro' [the] part muddy bottom to Hawkins', where [we] stop for breakfast. Meet Haggarty moving to Sangamon, then drive on to Barrows', 7 miles from Hindostan and encamp. 19 miles today.

14th (Friday) Drive 7 miles to [a] ferry on the east fork of the White River at Hindostan (pay $1.62½ for crossing), then proceed 3 miles [on a] bad road to [the] first house and stop for breakfast. In [the] evening [we] start on, cross the very bad, high hill road to Lewis', where [we] encamp on a hill. 15 miles today.

15th (Saturday) Start very early. Proceed 2 or 3 miles when one of the wagon wheels gives way and we are stopped, trying to brace it up with false spokes. After we get it fixed we proceed a short distance to a house, James Foyle's, where Mother has stopped. She was complaining of being unwell yesterday evening. Today she is too bad to proceed further, [and] was taken with a fainty fit soon after she got to the house. We encamp and wait till night to travel.

16th (Sunday) A fine, clear morning. Mother is still too unwell to travel. In the evening [we] find her very bad, and send one Thomas Leonard to Paoli for a Doctor Blanchard who reaches here about sunrise.

17th (Monday) [The doctor] gives her a dose of epicac, considers her case not dangerous, stays an hour and goes home. Mother is not relieved by the medicine, but continues sick and puking.

18th (Tuesday) She is still very sick [and] puking; takes castor oil which operates and stops [the] puking. We hoe corn.

19th (Wednesday) She is a little better. Heavy rain [today].

20th (Thursday) Go to Paoli to the doctor. He thinks it unnecessary to visit her; get some little medicine and return. Find her very bad, in a violent fever.

21st (Friday) A little easier but still very bad. Today we take the forewheel of the wagon and go about 10 miles to Squire Shield's for corn. We return back about 4 or 5 miles on the other road. I get 16 bushels [of] corn and return to camp at nightfall.

22d (Saturday) A clear fine day. Finish hoeing corn for Foyle's. Mother much the same as yesterday.

23d (Sunday) Rain. Mother worse at night, [in a] very bad violent fever, and pressure and burning in breast. Sit up with her.

24th (Monday) Very low in the morning, scarce any pulse. [Brother] Thomas goes for the doctor. [It] appears like she would not live till he returned. The doctor arrives late in the evening [and] finds her lower than he expected. [He] gives her wine, which a little revives her; continues giving her wine in small portions all night. She appears to be very easy, but very low; the cold sweat which she has been in all day has left her and she has recovered warmth in her extremities, which were cold. Have some small hopes.

25th (Tuesday) This morning she appears some little better and takes some medicine (barks), about 9 or 10 o'clock. [She is] very drowsy and sleepy. [In the] afternoon [she] appears to [be] fairly exhausted. [She] has taken no nourishment since taken sick. I quit giving her medicine, considering it useless. About 3 o'clock [it] appears as if she was dying, but soon comes to and appears better. Takes a few spoonfuls of buttermilk. It makes her sick. She strains to puke, does puke a little, [and] continues sick. Death now is very visible; she appears easy and composed, [and] is sensible to her situation. [She] gives directions about her burying clothes, and wants the black woman to sing a hymn for her. We send for a minister, a Mr. Byrum, 9 miles off; it is dark when he arrives. By then she is speechless; he prays by her bedside after which she attempts to speak, and, I think, calls [brother] Thomas. I ask her what she wants. She reaches me her cold hand and faintly articulates farewell. She gives her hand to each of the other boys and shortly after breathes her last, without groan, about 10 o'clock at night.

26th (Wednesday) Remain at camp nearly all day; [I] write a letter to Mr. Woods. About 4 o'clock in the afternoon the coffin is brought. Mr. Byrum delivers a very feeling discourse from some verses of the 23d Chapter of *Genesis* where the death of Sarah is mentioned, which is very suitable to the present case.

27th (Thursday) Left our camp at Foyle's with melancholy, and bid *adieu* to the last solitary home of her who has so long been the life of our company. We proceed 9 miles to Rev. Byrum's and stop and feed. From thence we proceed 3 miles further and encamp 3 miles west of N. Orleans where another wagon in encamped moving to the Wabash. Traveled 12 miles today.

28th (Friday) Pass thro' the village of Orleans, it is situated on a level or rather rolling land, some good farms immediately round it. From thence the land is rather hilly and broken for some distance to Lost River on which are some good farms. The soil is close, heavy and rather clayey but produces wheat, etc, very well, [and is] very natural to grass. We continue up Lost Creek several miles, then cross some ridges over to another creek, where we encamp at a large good limestone spring. 23 miles today.

29th (Saturday) After passing into Salem, 1½ miles, and traveling a few miles this morning, the face of the country entirely changes to poor, broken, [and] thinly settled. We reach a place called the "knobs"; there is a very considerable hill to descend without any previous ascent, it is a chain of rough broken ridges, running cross the country, or rather the abrupt termination of the high country to the west. After descending the "knobs" and traveling a few miles further, the country again changes. It is chiefly low and marshy, with intervening hills, rough and steep. We cross several little creeks. The timber [is] mostly beech; near night we reach a little village called Vienna where we encamp with another mover (one Davis from Ellison's Prairie). There are two taverns with one or two more houses in the village, [on] some good land. 21 miles today.

30th (Sunday) Very early, just as we are ready to start, it comes on rain. We get in a waste house and stay till breakfast. The rain ceases. We then drive on 5 or 6 miles thro' rough beech hills to a waste house on the road—where we stop in consequence of a thundergust and very heavy rain. The rain ceases in 2 or 3 hours, and [we] proceed, on slippery and wet roads, to Lexington, which is a county seat. [The town] has some good buildings, chiefly of brick, 3 taverns and some stores. The country around [it] is tolerably rich, with some good farms. It is 10 miles from Vienna. From here we proceed thro' a good country, 8 miles, to Martin's (or Smoke's) tavern where we encamp on a little creek; 17 miles.

JULY 1822

1st (Monday) Drive 10 miles, on mostly good road. Descend river hills to Madison, where we stop and feed. Madison is on the north bank of the Ohio, [and] is handsomely situated. [It] is a considerable town, [with] many good, and some elegant, brick buildings. From here the road is bad till we ascend the river hills and then not good. We proceed 8 miles to Indian (Kentucky) Creek. It rains and we layover in [a] house; 18 miles today.

2d (Tuesday) Cross [the] creek, then [up] some hills. We fall over on another little creek, which we ascend till the head rise, a hill, and stop to feed. Just as we again start, a very heavy rain begins; it lasts for about an hour and then clears off. [We] descend a steep hill to Judge Cotton's mill, cross [the] creek and ascend another high, steep hill on which is the town of a Mr. Sterling. The road forks [here], the right hand going to Vevay, 2 miles distant on the Ohio; we proceed on to Jacksonville, 3 miles further and encamp. More rain; 15 miles.

3d (Wednesday) Start early; drive 11 miles and stop for breakfast and to feed. [Wait for] a heavy rain shower, after which we proceed on to the town of Hartford, on Langhey Creek. The country [is] hilly [and] broken on each side of [the] creek. Some mills at [the] town [are] digging for salt water. We ascend a long hill from the creek, and, as there is a heavy shower of rain coming on, we stop and camp in [a] barn. Get our horses into [a] stable [and] pay 50 cents Cwt. for hay, 12½ cents for [our] lodging.

4th (Thursday) As the roads are muddy and [the] hills steep and slippery, we do not start till after breakfast; we then proceed on to Hogan Creek on which [there] is a good water mill. The creek is high from here, [and] we have a very bad hill to ascend, long and steep, after which we soon enter the town of Wilmington. It has 2 taverns and is 5 miles distant from Hartford. Preparations are [being made] here to celebrate the day; we descend the hill to the east branch of [the] Hogan (which we cross), and proceed a small distance; while going down a long, steep hill, the lame wagon wheel again gives way. We get down the hill to a little creek, near one Johnson's, and stop to try and get it repaired. After some time I go back to Wilmington. The workman has no seasoned wood that is large enough for our wheel. [Brother] Thomas, who went back to [the] mill, returns and [we] go on to camp.

5th   (Friday) Fix up the old wheel again with false spokes and after [a] late breakfast [we] start on, fearful of the wheel breaking down before we can get to Lawrenceburg. We ascend the long hill and, [after] some distance, descend it to a small creek. [We] then ascend another on which we continue till [we] descend to Tanner's Creek, which is lately raised till it is too high to ford. After some time we get a ferry boat and cross over into N. Lawrenceburg, 5 miles from [our] camp at Johnson's. We then drive up 1½ miles to Hardensburg, to one old Rab, a Dutchman from Staunton, Virginia. [We] encamp in his field while he fills the wheel.

6th   (Saturday) While Rab is at work repairing [the] wheel, me and [brother] Thomas go down into old Lawrenceburg to have some horses' shoes removed. After we return and the wheel [is] finished we fix up and start [on] about 4 o'clock; pay Rab $2.87½ for [the] wheel. We go to N. Lawrenceburg which is on the hill (or second bottom) above the old tavern, from which it is separated by a small lake and bluff. The old town is immediately on the river. [It] has one good street running parallel with the river on which are good buildings, mostly brick. The rest of the town is scattering. It is the county seat of Dearborn and has a handsome brick court house, two stories, a large one-story Methodist Episcopal church founded in 1821 and C____ and etc. After leaving town we proceed 2 miles up the bank of the Ohio to the mouth of the Big Miami. It is too late to cross, and we encamp in an old boat on the point, at the corner of the three states of Indiana, Ohio, and Kentucky. [We] see a stern boat pass up river.

7th   (Sunday) Start very early; it is some time before all is ferry'd across into the state of Ohio. I drive the wagon 2 miles and stop; the boys are hunting cows which strayed off last night. It is afternoon when they come up with them. We then hitch in and start on, passing General Harrison's, 5 miles above the mouth of the Miami on the Ohio; from thence we continue partly up the river to one Lofter's, where we encamp on a little creek about dark. Some rain and thunder with lightning. 11 miles today.

8th   (Monday) Do not start till after breakfast, then proceed on up the river. [We] pass some good farms within half a mile of

Cincinnati, where we stop at a creek and feed. Remain several hours here [while] Jones goes into town. We are soon surrounded by people looking at the elk, and continue on thro' the town. [We] see but little of it; it is, however, a very considerable town, containing between 11,000 and 12,000 souls. [There are] three market houses, a court house, several churches, and a seminary, which is a large elegant building. Covington is on the opposite side of the river from Cincinnati, just below the mouth [of the] Licking River. [We go to] Newport (above Cincinnati) and encamp 2 miles below the mouth of the Little Miami. [We go] 16 miles today, [and] 21 miles from [the] mouth of [the] Big Miami to Cincinnati.

9th (Tuesday) Start early [in] a thick fog till we cross the Miami. We continue up the bottom to Newton, containing 2 taverns, a store and some other buildings. After leaving it we soon leave the bottom and get on the beach flats. [We] cross several little creeks to Batavia on the east fork of the Little Miami, which we cross on a large frame bridge. We then ascend some hills to the beach flats on which we continue (the road mostly causeways) till night, when we encamp on a small branch in the woods 2 miles west of Williamsburg. 21 miles today.

10th (Wednesday) Start early, pass a broken bridge, [and] drive into Williamsburg, which is also situated on the east fork of the Little Miami. It contains some good buildings, mostly brick. Some however are of wood and stone. After leaving [the] creek we ascend a hill (which is commonly the case at all the creeks), into [the] beach flats; the road [is] mostly wet and causewayed; many of the creeks, branches, and bridges are swept away or tore up by the late freshets. We have some difficulty in getting round one where we stop and feed. One of our horses (Bob) was taken sick yesterday evening with a scour [and now] appears worse, [and] we give him a half dozen raw eggs. [We] proceed on across another little creek with [a] muddy bottom, pass a house, and enter [a] swamp, through which the road is chiefly all causewayed. [It is] 3 miles to White Creek which we cross on a good frame bridge. There are some farms along this creek. About 7 miles below here is a settlement of several hundred free negroes. We proceed about a mile to one Hutsinpiler's and encamp before night. Great appearance of rain. [We] drench our sick horse with salt and coat; he is like to die. 15 miles today.

11th (Thursday) Last night it began to rain very heavy and continues this morning, in consequence of which we do not start but remain encamped. Some go to the house and stay. The sick horse that I thought was dying last night is still alive, but very far spent. He staggers as he sways, and about 9 o'clock he dies, which adds another item to our misfortunes. It brings past scenes fresh to memory. Our situation is unpleasant, the day gloomy and reflections as discolored. Can see no prospect of much earthly pleasure. Misfortunes of the severest [kind have] already overtaken us; what more awaits we do not know; that we have difficulties to encounter is certain in this wilderness where scarce a ray of comfort pierces its gloomy shadows; but those reflections are painful. It has ceased raining about 1 or 2 o'clock, and we dry some of our plunder.

12th (Friday) Thick fog this morning, [and the] appearance of rain. It is late before we start. [We] continue thro' the swamp 6 miles to a mill at [the] first house. The road [is] very muddy and wet, some rain. Here we leave [the] swamp and take [a] hill 4 miles to Newmarket, a small village where [there] is a post office; from thence we proceed about 5 miles further over poor hills and bad road to a waste house where we encamp, having traveled about 15 miles.

13th (Saturday) Start after breakfast [and] proceed about 5 miles when it begins to rain. I look for [my] greatcoat and find [I] have left it at Hutsenpiler's; [Brother] Thomas goes back after it. We continue on about a mile to a creek and find it raised too high from today's rain to cross without [water] running into [the] wagon. Fortune appears to work against us, and we are again detained, waiting till the creek falls [so] that we may cross. About an hour later, by the sun, the creek has fallen so that we cross; we proceed a mile and half, after repairing some bridges, to a little creek where [we] stop to encamp till morning. 8 miles today.

14th (Sunday) Prepare to start very early, [but] find one of our horses (Jack) is sick. We delay starting, drench [the] horse and about 4 o'clock proceed on a mile [where we] meet Thomas (who had taken the Hillsborough road and gone as far as Bainbridge and returned to meet us). We proceed 4½ miles and encamp in a lane in [the] Limestone road.

15th (Monday) Proceed on good road 6 miles to Bainbridge, situated in Paint Creek bottom 2 miles above the ford, which we reach about 10 or 11 o'clock. But it is too high to ford, [and] we are detained from crossing till 1 or 2. The ferry boat is not good and the ferryman [is] afraid to take the wagon in; after some persuasion, however, he takes her in [and] we cross in safety. [We] proceed a mile down the creek and stop an hour. The road continues partly down the creek. The bottoms are a considerable width, rich and level. About sunset we cross a small creek, ascend a hill and encamp where we have an extended view of the bottom, a large portion [of which is] in cultivation. 18 miles.

16th (Tuesday) Start after breakfast, and drive 6 miles to Chillicothe, which is situated on a plain near the confluence of the Sciota River and Paint Creek. It is half a mile between them here, but the Sciota makes a great bend and the Paint is wider below. The city is laid [out] in the same plan as Philadelphia. It contains many good buildings, mostly of brick. Among the public buildings are a court house, several churches, and a steam mill with wool carding and spinning machines. There is a bridge constructed across the Sciota, which is worthy of notice. It is nearly ¼ mile long, [and is] partly covered over. It cost $54,000, and is [located] on the Lancaster road. Chillicothe contains a population of about 3,000. We soon arrive, pass several houses in the town, and proceed 4 miles down the bottom, cross the Sciota and encamp, having traveled about 10 miles today.

17th (Wednesday) Started early [in] a thick fog. Proceed on 10 miles to Richmond on a good level road. Here we cross the Salt Creek. Just below, two mills, a saw mill and a grist mill, were erected, one on each side [of the] creek. From here the road is hillier, tho' not steep. We fall over on to one fork of Salt Creek and continue up it, crossing it several times. In the evening encamp on it 4 miles west of Jackson, having traveled 20 miles.

18th (Thursday) Start early as usual. Cross some tolerably steep hills, and pass a place where salt has been made; there are several salt establishments in this neighborhood, at the head of the creek to which they have given name, and around the town of Jackson, which is on a hill near the creek. [Jackson] contains 3 taverns (always the first establishments in the western country towns). After leaving Jackson we continue thro' rather a poor broken country to Judge Poor's mill. From here the road is hilly and steep; we ascend a range of hills 4 or 5 miles, and encamp on a high one where water is scarce. 18 miles today.

19th (Friday) Start early, descend the hill on to a little creek, which we continue along down 4 or 5 miles to Blagg's tavern. We cross some hills and fall over onto Raccoon, a creek of a considerable size, which we cross on a high bridge. [We] pass a carding machine erected on the creek. We continue some distance down it, then cross some hills over on to a small creek where we stop and feed about 3 miles from Uncle Samuel Campbell's. We turn off the Chillicothe road, cross some hills to the Portsmouth road at Waddell's and Uncle Samuel's. 15 miles. In [the] evening [we] reach Uncle Samuel's. My relations all [seem] strange to me. I go to James Graham's [a cousin] and encamp.

20th (Saturday) Go to Gallipolis, to [the] quarterly meeting (Methodist). After dinner [I] cross the Ohio River—and am once more in Virginia after an absence of nearly 3 years.

21st (Sunday) Again attend preaching [in] Gallipolis. The large church is crowded with people. A Mr. Young preaches. After the first sermon is over, [I] go out by Graham's and from thence to Uncle Samuel's in company with James and Nancy [*neé* Campbell] Graham.

22d (Monday) Go home with [cousin] John Campbell; he goes on to work and I return and remain at my uncle's with cousin Nancy. At night I go and stay at John's.

23d (Tuesday) Go with John across Raccoon Creek to William Coulter's, [and] from thence to [cousin] Samuel Campbell's to run some lines for him. Stay all night with Samuel.

24th (Wednesday) After breakfast I start back. Go as far as Coulter's where John is waiting for me; we then go and run some lines for Coulter and after dinner [I] go with one Alexander Boggs and run ½ quarter for him for which he was to pay $1.50 but has not done it. In the evening go back to Coulter's and remain there all night, sit up late.

25th (Thursday) Return to uncle's and find them about starting. I put it off a day longer in consequence of providing some necessaries for [the] journey. In evening [I] go in company with John up to cousin James Campbell's, [but] he is not at home. He has a large family (7 children), which exhibit rather the marks of poverty. We go to one James' and from thence back by Graham's, where I stay all night.

26th (Friday) In morning [I] start back and breakfast rather unpleasantly with [cousin] John, after which [I] go again to uncle's. Nancy is there, [and I] remain all day. In [the] evening [I am] not very well, have a dysentery, and at night am very sick; a draught of mint tea of service.

27th (Saturday) Some better this morning. After breakfast [we] take leave of our friends and proceed on [our] journey. It is 8 miles to Gallipolis where we stop to lay in some stores. Meet with old Mr. Rees [another relation] in town, who insists on us going up with him and staying a day or two. After some time we conclude to go there; it is 4 miles above Gallipolis. A shower of rain before night.

28th (Sunday) Spend some time inquiring a way to get into [the] Valley Road by crossing here. I go across the Ohio at the mouth of [the] Kanawha and examine a hill (which is said to be the worst in the road till we get into the Gallipolis Road); [it] is bad but I think it is practicable to take a wagon over it. Go back to Rees's and remain there till after dinner, first taking the wagon down the bank (by hand) and the horses across the river. We then take the wagon over, and about 3 or 4 o'clock are all once more safely landed in Virginia. Take leave of the balance of our friends, cross the bottom about a mile and take the hill. After pulling up the steepest [part], the road is too narrow for all the horses to pull. The wagon gets down off the road, from which place we are unable to move her till we take out a great part of the load and prize her up into [the] road. We then go up to the top of the hill and encamp one mile or a little upwards from the Ohio.

29th (Monday) Start early, the road narrow and rough, [and go] 5 miles on to a little creek where several families are settled. From hence it is 4 miles into [the] Valley or Gallipolis Road. We cross some steep hills and fall over onto another little creek which we [follow] down to the other road. Just above [it] we stop and feed and breakfast. It is near 2 o'clock; much fallen timber in the road kept us later. After feeding we proceed, pass one house, and ascend a very steep hill, which takes up some time; afterwards the road runs pretty much on a ridge and [is] tolerable good. [It is] 6 miles to [the] next house. We arrive after sunset and encamp at the foot of a hill where water is scarce, having come 15 miles [on a] bad road.

30th (Tuesday) Cross a hill, [and go] one mile to [the] next house; from thence it is 7 miles to [the] next. We cross several hills [and] fall over on a creek. [We] keep down it several miles [and] cross another ridge to McCollister's where [we] stop and feed (pay 62½ cents a bushel for oats). From here the road is hilly and rough to Hurricane Creek. We descend a very steep hill to [the] Creek and keep down it one mile to [the] first house, 8 miles from McCollister's. It is night before we get there; we pass one house and encamp at the second. 16 miles today.

31st (Wednesday) Ascend a hill from the creek, after which the road is tolerable good [for] 5 miles into Teaze's Valley at Hanley's. We proceed up the valley 3 or 4 miles and stop and feed. Some rain. Then continue on to Cole Mountain which we cross, [then] ferry [the] Cole at the mouth. Proceed a mile and encamp in a schoolhouse on the banks of [the] Kanawha. 15 miles today.

AUGUST 1822

1st (Thursday) Some appearance of rain. We proceed up the Kanawha 3 or 4 miles. The road then leaves the bottom, crosses the points of ridges, [and is] very bad from our old camp at Mattick's for some miles. We again get into the road [beside] a little creek with steep banks where we stop and feed. We proceed some distance. The weather [is] excessive warm, [and] it begins to rain very heavy. For half an hour we shelter under a beech tree. We then proceed [on a] bad, muddy road chiefly along the river bank, from which we can discern many hands at work clearing out a channel in the river just below and at the Elk Shoals below Charleston. We encamp 2 miles above Charleston, [having come] 14 or 13 miles today. More rain tonight.

2d (Friday) Cloudy and dull, [and] like for rain. The road [is] sloppy and bad. We proceed on among the licks. They [have] discovered a method of boiling with a coal fire; there is plenty of coal in the hills along the river. In the evening [we] cross Cabin Creek (another of our old encampments), proceed 2 miles and encamp. 17 miles. See McKorkle, etc.

3d (Saturday) Continue on up the river [and] pass the upper lick, two miles below Jones' ferry [on a] narrow bad road; stop and feed opposite Daniel Curry's. He comes over to us. In the evening [we] cross Armstrong's Creek, just below Major Buster's, another of our old encampments. We proceed on and cross Loup Creek where the road is very bad and, in a mile, encamp at one end of a lane 3 miles below the falls. [The] mountains [here] appear like they had shut in the river so close that it has only a narrow passage. About 12 or 15 miles today.

4th (Sunday) Continue along the river, the road narrow and bad; in 3 miles [we] reach Montgomery's, near the falls, where the road leaves the river and goes up the side of a bad, rocky hill and a little overhang with precipices. Two miles up the draft there is a man settled (one Masterson); from thence it is 1¼ miles to the top of Cotton Hill, the road mostly steep and narrow. The weather [is] not quite so warm as on the Kanawha. A little cloudy, but notwithstanding, we are a considerable time in ascending the hill. The east side is not so long. After descending it we stop and feed, then cross Laurel Run (another old encampment). [We] stop at [the] first house and encamp about dark on a small branch, 5 or 6 miles from the falls. Rain tonight; 9 miles.

5th (Monday) The road [is] somewhat bad from the late rain; the weather [is] quite cool. We proceed thro' the Loup 13 miles to the top of [the] North River cliffs, where we encamp before night at a waste place (one of our old encampments). Weather quite cold, near frost.

6th (Tuesday) Start very early [on a] cool morning. Descend the cliffs [on] a dismal road [for] a mile to [the] North River. It is 8 or 9 o'clock when we get ferry'd over and begin slowly to ascend the cliffs. [We] expect difficulty as several of the horses are lame. About noon or a little later, [we] reach the top. [I] stop and feed, then proceed on to Tyry's [Teary?] at [the] top of [the] mountain and encamp, having come 7 miles today. The weather [is] cool, which is much in our favor. The night [is] cold and windy. A drove of horses from the Ohio stops here.

7th (Wednesday) Still cool. We proceed on early, pass thro' the Shades of Death and stop a mile short of the top of Suel [Mountain] and feed. [We] proceed on past a farm on top of the mountain, then descend it. [We] pass Teary's, on to Alderson's at [the] fork of [the] road (an old camp), where [we] encamp. About 17 miles.

8th (Thursday) Cloudy and like for rain; we proceed on thro' the meadows, [and] cross [a] creek on a long bridge. [We go over] some bad hills, [and encounter] a little rain. About noon [we] reach the top of the meadow mountain 10 miles, and stop and feed at Young's, then descend it, pass Chrys's {Chris?], where part of the new turnpike road [has been] finished. We drive a mile on it to Hannah's, and, after passing Pearsy's, take the left hand road, descending a steep hill to Robert Rennick's. Cannot get grain of him. [We] proceed on half a mile and stop at dark, where one of Rennick's men overtakes us with an invitation to return. We do not immediately accept it, and he sends his son and requests us to bring all our horses back, which we do and we go and stay with him. 17 miles today.

9th (Friday) Proceed on thro' a good settlement in the Big Levels to Frankfort (10 miles), where get [we] oats at 2/3. Then [we go] 3 miles to Burns' mill on Spring Creek, where we stop and feed and get some meal ground. There is a good bridge here, built across Spring Creek on wooden piers, filled with stone and well secured by braces. After crossing [the] creek we have, as is usual, a hill to ascend, after which the road is tolerably good, the country [is] rolling, [and] a great proportion [of it is] in a state of cultivation, [with] extensive farms. Late in the evening we pass the residence of Major Rennick, *deceased*, some distance off to the left hand side of the road. The dwelling is of stone, large and 3 stories high. The Major, at his death, bequeathed it to his niece, the daughter of Robert Rennick, who has married a person of the same name, a distant relative, [and] who is the present owner of the place. Father and Jones [go] there and [stay] all night. We stop a short distance from there and encamp on a hill just above a good spring of water, having traveled about 15 miles.

10th (Saturday) Proceed on early, [and] pass the residence of William Brown, a distant relative of my mother's. When he discovers who we are [he] is glad to see us, but disappointed when he hears of mother's death. They accompany us as far as Benjamin Irvine's expecting to see father; he has gone on and they are disappointed and return. I proceed on a little, [then] stop [in the] afternoon and feed. [I] then pass along Droop Mountain into the little levels, [and] cross Locust Creek on a rotten crazy bridge. From here it is 3 miles to Jourden's

[Jorden], near where [there] is a camp meeting. It is late in the evening when we reach there [and] a numerous company comes out to meet us. Some [are] acquaintances, but most [come] to see the elk. We cross a branch after passing Jorden's and encamp on a hill about ¼ mile from the meeting [which we visit that] night. A considerable congregation and much stir amongst them; about 11 o'clock [we] return to camp, however.

11th (Sunday) Start early, not however, before people begin to gather about us to see the elk. Pass Major Poag's in one mile; he comes out to see father [and] attends us a mile. We then proceed to Cackley's, [where we] stop to try to get grain, [but] cannot get any. Proceed a mile further, pass William Bradshaw's, and stop at [the] forks of road. Go off to William Cackley's plantation and get enough sheaf oats to feed at night, then proceed on, the weather warm. Cross Greenbrier River, go up Beaver Creek, and cross it several times. Late in evening pass Cummins' and encamp. 15 miles today.

12th (Monday) Start early [in] a thick fog this morning. Stop at Perkins' and get grain. Pass Bradshaw's (the county seat of Pocahontas), and take [the] right hand road up thro' the gap, which is immensely rocky. We stop on Lockridge's plantation and feed, then proceed on up Knap's Creek to John Moor's where we encamp, having travelled 14 miles about.

13th (Tuesday) Start early, pass Levi Moor's, stop near the old cabins to feed, then cross the mountain. Every part of the road [is now] quite familiar. We reach Back Creek about 3 o'clock. Acquaintanances [are] now at every house. We stop at Frederick Bire's before night and encamp. He is very clever.

14th (Wednesday) A little cloudy and some appearance of rain. We proceed on after breakfast, full of the idea of home and that this is our last day's travel of so long a journey; we stop at Mr. Woods'. Him and his lady attend(s us) [to our] home; they had previously heard of us and put the house in order for our reception. We reach it about afternoon, perhaps one or two o'clock; the place looks somewhat desolate, the house being unoccupied and the garden grown up with weeds.

V.

A DESCRIPTION OF THE
CITY OF CINCINNATI IN 1822

Cincinnati is [the] seat of justice for Hamilton County, [and is located] 20 miles from the mouth of the G. Miami at [the] S. W. corner. It was laid off in the year 1788 around Fort Washington and settled by Yankees, but did not extensively improve till after General Wayne's defeat of the Indians in 1794; but, subsequent to that period, it, together with the adjacent country, has rapidly progressed. In July 1815 it contained about 1,100 buildings [consisting of] 660 dwellings, the rest stores, shops, etc. The population was then 6,500; at present it has increased to upwards of 11,000 and public improvements [are] in proportion. There are about 60 common mercantile stores, some of which do wholesale business, besides about 10 book, drug, iron, and shoe stores.

Among the public buildings are Presbyterian, Baptist, Methodist, and Friends meeting houses, all of brick. That for [the] Presbyterian has been lately erected on Main Street, and is an elegant structure, 85 by 68 feet on the ground and 50 feet high to the cornices or eaves. The Baptist meeting house is also a handsome building, 55 by 40 [feet in] area. The Lancasterian school house consists of two oblong wings 30 feet apart, each 80 feet deep with a connecting building of 30 by 18 feet (which contains the staircases leading to the second stories). One of the wings is designed for boys and the other for girls. Within 2 weeks after opening the school upwards of 400 scholars were admitted, and the building is calculated to accommodate 1100.

The court house is a commodious building 62 feet long and 56 broad, connected with what are the necessary offices, [and] made fire proof. There are 3 brick market houses abundantly supplied, one of which has been recently built upon 3 rows of pillars and is 300 feet long. A most stupendous large building of stone is likewise erected on the bank of the Ohio for a steam mill. It is 9 stories high at the water's edge and is 87 feet long by 62 feet broad. The engine is one of 70 horse power and is designed to drive 4 pair of stones, beside an oil pulling and several other mills. Left [my] watch at Vickary's near Edwardsville.

APPENDIX

Copy of a letter from James Brown Campbell to Mr. Shields, for whom he worked during the summer of 1821:

Dear Shields:

On closing on the old range line between 10 and 11 W., I find it has been badly run. My E. random between 25 or 36' intersected it in 72 chains, 400 lks. N. of the corner. I have run 1 mile of the range, the first 35:50 chains I fell 800 lks. E. of the ¼ Sec. corner. I removed 5 C 50 N. and established the corner on the old line. In running the other half I nearly followed the line, only fell 6 or 8 lks. W. of Sec. corner, to which it was 76 chains. I also removed it the 4 chains N., thinking it proper to call it an outmiss.

I am at a loss how to proceed—whether to measure all the lines over or whether to remove the corners on out; on each mile the last, will make bad closes on it. To measure it over there will not be an outs difference for any of the other miles; the difference in the measure (about 100 lks. in a mile) will, if we measure down, leave the last corner still north of our own—or the last mile on R line will be full long for our measure without removing the corner.

If the Township N. would not run, I believe it would be right to depart so far from the general practice as to run the line all over and establish corners within proper distances and on a true line; but as the one N. is surveyed, I do not know whether it will be a proper course to correct it.

I have run up the first tier and dropped part, ran down 35 chains and left it until I can hear from you first. Excuse this (I fear unintelligible scrawl) as I am in a great hurry.

Truly yours,

J. Campbell

NAME INDEX

PLACE INDEX

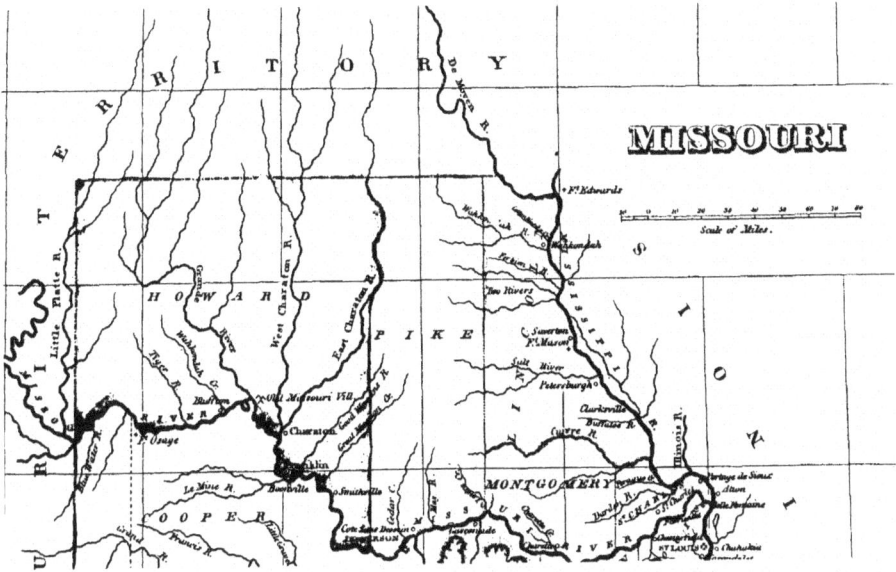

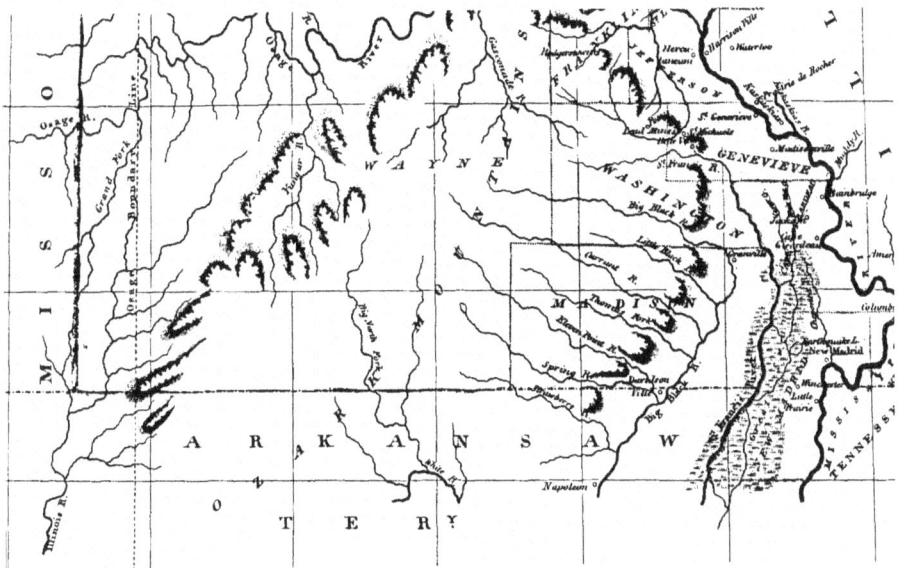

www.ingramcontent.com/pod-product-compliance
Lightning Source LLC
LaVergne TN
LVHW011333080426
835513LV00006B/313